ACADEMICALLY SPEAKING

WADSWORTH ENGLISH FOR ACADEMIC PURPOSES SERIES

Charles H. Blatchford and Jerry L. Messec, Series Editors

Available in 1987

Academically Speaking Janet L. Kayfetz and Randy L. Stice

Academic Writing Workshop Sarah Benesch, Mia Rakijas, and Betsy Rorschach

Overheard and Understood Sharon Bode and Sandra Moulding Lee

Understanding Conversations Catherine Tansey and Charles H. Blatchford

Write On! Patricia Byrd

Academically Speaking

Janet L. Kayfetz
University of California, Santa Barbara

Randy L. Stice
University of California, Santa Barbara

Heinle & Heinle Publishers
A Division of Wadsworth, Inc.
Boston, Massachusetts 02116

English/ESL Editor: John Strohmeier
Editorial Assistants: Holly Allen, Sharon McNally
Production Editor: Deborah O. McDaniel
Designer: Andrew H. Ogus
Print Buyer: Barbara Britton
Copy Editor: Bob Seitz
Cover: Andrew H. Ogus
Cover Illustration: Jeanne Schreiber

Heinle & Heinle Publishers is a division of Wadsworth, Inc.

Printed in the United States of America   49

        8 9 10--96 95

Library of Congress Cataloging-in-Publication Data

Kayfetz, Janet L.
  Academically speaking.

  (Wadsworth English for academic purposes series)
    1. English language—Text-books for foreign speakers.
2. English language—Spoken English.   3. English
language—Technical English.   4. Public speaking.
I. Stice, Randy L.   II. Title.   III. Series.
PE1128.K384   1987   428.3'4   86-30765
ISBN 0-534-08004-9

Contents

Chapter 2/Interpreting Graphs and Tables   15

Chapter 3/Defining Terms   35

UNIT TWO/ DISCUSSING INFORMATION   49

Chapter 4/Discussing an Article   50

Chapter 5/Lecture and Discussion Section 63

UNIT THREE/ PRESENTING INFORMATION 73

Chapter 6/Process Speech 74

Chapter 7/Impromptu Speech   87

Why Practice the Impromptu Speech?   87
Assignment Overview   88
Useful Expressions   88
Assignment 1: Understanding the Article   88
"Environmental Ethics"   89
Guidelines for the Impromptu Speech   91
How Long Should You Speak?   91
Assignment 2: Giving the Impromptu Speech   91
Worksheet 1: Impromptu Speech   93

UNIT FOUR/ PRESENTING AND DEFENDING A POSITION   95

Chapter 8/Panel   96

What Is a Panel?   96
Why Practice a Panel?   97
Assignment Overview   97
Useful Expressions   97
Topics   98
Choosing a Topic and Forming Your Panel   99
Assignment 1: Preparation   100
Guidelines for the Panel Moderator   100
Assignment 2: Practice   101
Assignment 3: Introductions   101
Assignment 4: Presentation   102
Guidelines for Panel Audience Members   102
Worksheet 1: Preparing an Introduction   103

Chapter 9/Seminar   104

What Is a Seminar?   104
What Is the Difference between a Seminar and a Panel?   105
Why Practice the Seminar?   105

Chapter 10/Challenging and Defending a Position   123

About the Wadsworth EAP Series

The Wadsworth English for Academic Purposes (EAP) series was conceived to provide appropriate teaching materials for college courses that focus on the academic uses of English. The eighteen texts of the EAP series are designed to help ESL students achieve communicative competence in all aspects of academic life in the United States. These materials teach the skills of reading, writing, listening, and speaking and can be used for either intensive or nonintensive formats, in classrooms or for individual study, and for courses of varying lengths.

The Wadsworth EAP series is based on three principles:

1. *Comprehensive skills development:* Because the EAP program is based on the philosophy that language is an integrated unity, each book not only stands on its own but also prepares for and builds on other texts in the series. Individual skills are explored in depth at three distinct levels of proficiency; topics across all skill levels retain a consistent yet nonrepetitive approach.

2. *Academic community context:* The Wadsworth EAP series prepares students for the varied language uses they will encounter daily in their academic careers. All teaching and learning activities are set in the context of college or university classes; however, some texts go even further to depict the extended academic community. This context-specific approach assumes that students possess the learning skills and educational background typically found at academic English centers.

3. *Student-centered, process-oriented materials:* Each text in the Wadsworth EAP series places student learning activities at the heart of each lesson, requiring students to take an active responsibility for their role in the learning process.

The components of the Wadsworth EAP program will include:

Three grammar practice books that encourage students to practice language appropriate to specific academic contexts.

Six listening comprehension texts and tapes that develop (a) listening skills to the level needed for achievement in an academic program and (b) appreciation of the social situations students will experience in the extended academic community.

Three oral language books whose progressive communicative activities develop the spoken language skills necessary for students in U.S. campus communities.

Three reading skill development books that help students acquire skills for reading authentic English texts within the academic community context.

Three progressive process-oriented writing texts that develop writing skills from practice with the Latin alphabet (for those unfamiliar with the system) to communicative writing to writing based on individual research. Writing assignments are based on both visual and written situations. Higher-level texts provide instruction and practice in summarizing articles and research as well as in preparing longer papers. All three books combine practice in composing and editing to the degree necessary to express ideas logically and clearly.

The authors of the Wadsworth EAP series have developed their materials based on teaching experience, but the series is not teacher-proof; it will not work for someone who expects all the answers and a strict step-by-step approach. Each text is designed to allow instructors the flexibility to use their own teaching schemes, styles, and techniques. Not providing all "correct" answers reflects current trends in ESL teaching, which focus on the student as a developing being, struggling to construct, to decipher, and to negotiate meaning. Some texts do provide answer keys, however, as a help to students who may be using the text on their own.

Although no textbook is ideal for all students (or all teachers), this program will work for everyone who is willing to participate fully in classes and assignments. The texts are intended to broaden the students' vision and empower them with the expanding possibilities of language. Control and support are found not only in the materials themselves but also in the teachers who guide the students through them. Just as students can learn to make language their servant, so can instructors learn to make the materials support their individual pedagogical goals.

In sum, the Wadsworth EAP series does more than simply prepare students for a grammar-based examination; the program can help international students master communication in academic English through meaningful practice in the American academic context. The student-centered materials shift the responsibility for learning from the teacher to the student, who, in the process, is provided the opportunity to fulfill his or her potential. And isn't that what each of us would like to achieve?

Charles H. Blatchford and Jerry L. Messec,
Series Editors

Preface

This book is designed to give students an introduction to and practice in using *academic English*. We have identified and described specific settings in which students use the academic register, and we have designed activities to familiarize them with the rules and the quality of performance expected in these settings. Although we have chosen activities that are applicable to specific academic situations, the activities will prepare students for language use in the extended academic community as well. The philosophical and pedagogical implications of these goals are twofold:

1. The text is activity centered rather than information centered.

2. The text is student centered rather than teacher centered.

An Activity-Centered Text

The fact that this book is activity centered has four ramifications.

1. The primary concern is what the students can do rather than what they know. For this reason, the majority of the text is devoted to activities rather than to information about the activities.

2. Because nearly all authentic academic speech situations involve readings and integrate the four language skills (listening, speaking, reading, writing), several chapters are based on readings, and many activities integrate all four skills.

3. Because the different speech situations suggest a different format for each assignment, you will find some variation in the structure of the activities from chapter to chapter. Even so, most activities have a threefold structure: *preparation, practice,* and *presentation.*

4. The book is process centered at every level—from the steps within a given activity, to the sequence of activities within a given chapter, to the sequence of chapters within a unit, and finally to the ordering of the units within the book.

A Student-Centered Text

The student-centered focus of the book is reflected in the fact that most of the class time involves students working in pairs or in small groups with little direct involvement from the teacher. Consequently, the students have significant responsibility for the success or failure of a given activity and of the class in general. This raises the immediate concern of student motivation and the larger issue of the roles of the teacher and the student in an activity-centered and student-centered course.

The Role of the Teacher

Of these concerns, the most important is the role of the teacher. For this text, the teacher's role is primarily that of facilitator. We understand facilitating to consist of the following:

1. *Setting up the activity,* whether this means simply organizing students into pairs or small groups or setting up a debate or panel discussion. The amount of out-of-class preparation that this requires will vary considerably from chapter to chapter and even from assignment to assignment. Dividing students into groups to discuss an article or to analyze an analogy will require considerably less preparation than will delivering a lecture or setting up an impromptu speech.

2. *Setting time limits* for each activity or portion of an activity.

3. *Circulating around the room*, particularly during pair and small-group assignments, to stimulate discussion and answer questions.

4. *Monitoring the progress of an activity:*
   a. Are the students staying on the topic?
   b. Are they working toward the goal of the activity?
   c. Are they staying within the allotted time?

5. *Providing feedback*, both formal and informal, oral and written, which can include any of the following:
   a. commenting on ideas and participation
   b. ensuring that, in a small group discussion, the leader of the group is following the guidelines provided
   c. ensuring that all members of a discussion group are following the guidelines for appropriate participation
   d. providing written feedback on the culminating activity of a given chapter, whether it be a speech, debate, or seminar

As suggested by the preceding guidelines, the teacher's role will change from chapter to chapter and from activity to activity. Some activities will require careful monitoring, but others will not; some will require significant preparation outside of class, but others will not; some will suggest verbal feedback, and others will suggest written feedback. It is important for teachers to be sensitive to these differences and to be aware of the flexibility inherent in our approach.

Adapting the Textbook to Yourself and Your Class

Every textbook will be adapted to the teacher's personality and abilities as well as to the personality and needs of the class. We have sought to design a text that recognizes and allows for this. The sequence of chapters and the sequence of activities within a chapter have been carefully planned. However, we strongly encourage freedom in (1) determining time limits and pace of the course, (2) adjusting topics and activities to fit different levels, (3) using the book for one semester or two, and (4) deciding whether to do certain preparatory activities at home or in class, orally or in writing.

Pair and small-group work are strongly emphasized throughout the book, and much of the success of this work hinges on the composition of the pairs or small groups. We have found that groups work most effectively when they are composed in advance for specific assignments, considering such factors as nationality, age, major, and familiarity. This is a crucial part of setting up any activity and should receive a commensurate amount of attention.

Presentations, both individual and group, followed by a question-and-answer period, are another activity frequently used in this text. When an activity involves a presentation before the entire class by either an individual student or a pair, it is not necessary for every student or pair to present. Teachers should feel free to limit the presentations to four or five. Be sure, though, that the same students do not make presentations each time. When there is a question-and-answer period, we have found that the period is more successful when specific students are told *before* the presentation that they must ask a question at its conclusion or when every student is told to prepare a question. After the presentation, the teacher usually calls on only two or three students to ask their questions.

The Role of the Student

The student's role in this course is also vitally important and centers on the following question: Where does student motivation come from in a student-centered course? It is our experience that student motivation for any course comes from three sources:

1. *The enthusiasm of the teacher.* A teacher who consistently shows confidence in and enthusiasm for a course is very likely to engender the same attitides in his or her students.

2. *The perceived usefulness of the assignment.* If students believe that a given activity will, either by itself or in sequence with other activities, help them develop necessary and desirable skills, their motivation for that activity will be enhanced. However, the primary responsibility for communicating the usefulness of a given activity lies with the teacher, and this may have to be done frequently.

3. *Interest in the topic.* If the topic for an activity interests students, is familiar to them, and is relevant to their experience, it will supply much of the motivation for the activity.

The ideal for every activity is that the students become so engrossed in it that they forget they are doing an ESL exercise and become concerned only with the efficacy of their communication. And that, after all, is our common goal.

Acknowledgments

We would like to extend our thanks to several people whose assistance made this book possible. Thanks go first to Nancy Marwin, Kim McNeill, and Richard Nettell, our colleagues in the English as a Second Language Program at the University of California, Santa Barbara, who used and critiqued numerous versions of the manuscript. We would also like to express our appreciation to Charlie Blatchford for his personal encouragement as well as his detailed and insightful comments on the manuscript and to Jerry Messec, who helped us formulate our original concept of this book. Next, we want to thank the staff at Wadsworth, particularly John Strohmeier, Debbie McDaniel, and Andrew Ogus, who worked closely with us to bring the book to its final form. Special thanks go to Becky Hanna, who tirelessly typed numerous versions of the manuscript and who always accommodated our deadlines. Finally, we wish to publicly acknowledge the shared growth and delight that illuminated this project and carried it to its completion.

January 1987

Janet L. Kayfetz
Randy L. Stice

UNIT ONE

Developing Academic Speech Skills

CHAPTER 1

Interviewing

Skills used in this chapter:
—asking questions
—answering questions
—organizing information
—taking notes
—reporting information

The purpose of this chapter is to practice asking and answering questions. You will do this by participating in and conducting interviews with one of your classmates and with an American acquaintance. You will then compile the information you gathered and report your findings to the entire class.

What Is an Interview?

An interview is a technique for gathering information. It is a structured conversation between two people on a particular topic. Newspaper and television reporters use the interview technique to elicit facts and statements from political figures, authors of books, and other people who are experts on a particular subject. Personnel and admissions officers also conduct interviews to gather information. The information collected in such interviews is used to write news reports, or to present information in other written documents or in oral reports.

Why Practice the Interview?

During your stay in the United States, you will have many opportunities to participate in an interview. Sometimes you will be the interviewer and ask the questions, and sometimes you will be the interviewee and answer questions. Here are a few examples of interview settings you may participate in:

1. Talking with a university representative about admission procedures and policies for entrance to graduate school, law school, medical school, and so on.

2. Talking with a professor in a private conference.

3. Talking with a personnel officer during the application procedure for a job, either on or off campus.

4. Talking with a news reporter during an interview about your country for a campus or local newspaper.

Assignment Overview

The activities in this chapter are closely linked. You will begin by preparing the questions you will ask in your interview. You will then interview one of your classmates and be interviewed by him. This will prepare you for the next step, which is to interview an American using the same set of questions. Finally, you will give a brief speech presenting the results of your two interviews.

Useful Expressions

I'd like to ask you a few questions on the subject of _____.

Could you tell me what you think of _____?

What is your opinion on _____?

Do you agree with the following statement? _____

Let me repeat my question.

Could you expand on that?

Could you repeat that?

Let me see if I understood you. You feel that _____.

(Continued)

3

Do you mean that _____?

Thank you very much for giving me your time. This has been very
interesting.

Assignment 1: Preparing Your Questions

In this assignment, you will prepare for an interview on the topic of
education.

1. Prepare a *minimum* of ten questions on the topic, using Worksheet
   1 on page 7. Although it is not necessary to memorize the
   questions, you should be very familiar with them. You may,
   however, refer to your notes during the interview.

2. You may wish to solicit opinions on the following broad issues:

   a. What is the goal of education: self-knowledge, knowledge of the
      world, a job, or status?

   b. Should students share the responsibility of deciding what is
      taught and how it is taught?

   c. Do most students choose instant solutions to assignments?

   d. Should universities have stricter entrance requirements?

Note: The questions above are *not* suitable interview questions; they are
too broad and are examples of general topics. The following are examples
of suitable interview questions:

   a. Should students in a composition class be allowed to choose
      their writing topics? Why or why not?

   b. Do you think that students in the physical sciences are more
      diligent than students in the social sciences? Why or why not?

   c. Are difficult assignments an indication of a good teacher or a
      bad teacher? Explain.

Assignment 2: Interviewing a Classmate

Now that you have prepared your questions, you are ready for the first
interview. You will have twenty-five minutes to conduct your interview.
Your teacher will assign you a partner and will tell you when twenty-five
minutes are up. Your partner will then have twenty-five minutes to
interview you.

   Familiarize yourself with the following guidelines.

Guidelines for the Interview

If you are the interviewer:

1. You may refer to the list of questions you prepared in Assignment 1.

2. Begin the interview by explaining your purpose.

3. If you do not understand the answer to one of your questions, ask the person to repeat it or clarify it.

4. Try not to talk too much.

5. Let the conversation run naturally. If you think of a new question during the interview, ask it.

6. Take notes during the interview. Use Worksheet 1 at the end of this chapter to record your notes.

7. After the interview, at home, read over your notes and prepare a summary of the interview at the bottom of the worksheet.

If you are the interviewee:

1. Give complete answers to the questions. Volunteer information.

2. Pay careful attention to the interviewer's questions. If you don't understand one, ask for clarification.

3. Before answering a difficult question, spend a few seconds collecting your thoughts.

Assignment 3: Interviewing an American

To complete your cross-cultural study of education, you are now going to interview an American using the same set of questions, instructions, and quidelines that you used in Assignment 2. Take notes on the worksheet.

Assignment 4: Speech Preparation

Having solicited the opinions of two culturally different people on a variety of educational issues, you are now going to give a short speech in which you highlight what you consider to be the most interesting similarities and differences between your two interviewees. Follow the guidelines below to prepare for a five-minute speech. Arrange your information in an outline using Worksheet 2.

1. Review the notes from your two interviews.

2. Prepare an introduction that includes the following information:
   a. the subject of the talk

    b. information about each of your interviewees: name, country, occupation, age, and sex

3. In the body of the talk, identify two or three points of similarity between the two interviewees and two or three points on which your interviewees differed.

4. Prepare the conclusion for your talk in which you discuss the implications of your findings for foreign students studying in the United States.

Assignment 5: Practice

1. Your teacher will assign you a partner *who was not your interviewee.*

2. Give your talk to your partner.

3. Your partner will make suggestions on how you can improve your talk. Incorporate them into your outline before you give your talk to the class.

4. Now your partner will give his talk, and you will make suggestions.

Assignment 6: Presentation

1. Your teacher will determine the order in which you will speak.

2. When you give your talk, you may refer to your outline. Be sure that your talk does not exceed five minutes. At the conclusion of your talk, there will be one minute for questions.

3. After your talk, give your outline to your teacher, who will make written comments on it about your content, organization, and presentation and return it to you.

Worksheet 1/Questions for the Interview

Name _____

Date _____

Use this worksheet to write down the questions you will use during your two interviews. Below each question, there is space for you to make notes on the responses from each of your interviewees. This arrangement will make it easier for you to compare and contrast the opinions of your two interviewees.

Question 1: _____

_____

Classmate's opinion   *American's opinion*

Question 2: _____

_____

Classmate's opinion   *American's opinion*

Question 3: _____

_____

Classmate's opinion   *American's opinion*

(Over)   **Chapter 1/Interviewing   7**

Question 4:_____

_____

Classmate's opinion   American's opinion

Question 5:_____

_____

Classmate's opinion   American's opinion

Question 6:_____

_____

Classmate's opinion   American's opinion

Question 7:_____

_____

Classmate's opinion   American's opinion

Question 8:_____

_____

Classmate's opinion   American's opinion

Question 9:_____

_____

Classmate's opinion   American's opinion

Question 10:_____

_____

Classmate's opinion   American's opinion

Worksheet 2/Speech Outline

Name

Date

Use the information from Worksheet 1 to complete this worksheet. You may refer to this worksheet during your speech. At the conclusion of your speech, give it to your teacher.

Introduction

A. Subject of the talk:

B. Background information about your interviewees:

   1. Name

   2. Country

   3. Occupation

   4. Age

   5. Sex

Body of the talk

A. Similarities

   1.

      a. Example:

      b. Example:

(Over)

2.

    a. Example:

    b. Example:

3.

    a. Example:

    b. Example:

B. Differences

  1.

    a. Example:

    b. Example:

  2.

    a. Example:

    b. Example:

  3.

    a. Example:

    b. Example:

Conclusion

Implications of your findings for foreign students studying in the United States.

A.

B.

C.

Teacher's Comments

Content:

Organization:

Presentation:

CHAPTER 2

Interpreting Graphs and Tables

Skills used in this chapter:
—asking questions
—answering questions
—gathering information
—discussing information
—organizing information into a graph or table
—reporting information

In this chapter, you will practice interpreting graphs and tables dealing with a variety of subjects. You will also gather information and organize it into an original graph or table.

Why Practice Interpreting Graphs and Tables?

In many academic disciplines, particularly the natural and social sciences, much information is presented graphically. You will find graphs and tables printed in textbooks, articles, research and laboratory reports, grant proposals, theses, and dissertations; they may also be part of various oral presentations such as seminars, lectures, conferences, and panels. For these reasons, it is essential that you be able to discuss data presented in these formats.

Assignment Overview

This chapter is divided into two parts: graphs and tables. Each part consists of an introduction, an example, and an assignment. In the final activity, you will construct your own graph or table and present it to the class.

Graphs

What Is a Graph?

A graph is a diagram that exhibits a relationship between two variables. Each variable is represented by one axis on the graph.

How Do You Interpret a Graph?

To understand a graph, you must answer the following questions:

1. What is the subject of the graph?

2. What do the horizontal and vertical axes represent?

3. What trend or pattern does the graph reveal?

4. What are the implications of the graph? What predictions can you make, or what conclusions can you draw?

Figure 1 is an illustration of how to interpret a graph.

1. *Subject of the graph:*
   This graph shows the growth of the population of the United States from 1790 to 1980 and estimates growth to 2050.

2. *Horizontal axis:*
   The horizontal axis represents years, with fifty-year intervals marked.
   Vertical axis:
   The vertical axis represents the population in units of 100 million.

3. *Trend or pattern:*
   The population of the United States began to increase dramatically around 1850 and continued to accelerate through 1980.

4. *Implications and predictions:*
   If this trend holds, the population of the United States will double itself between 1980 and 2050.

The complete interpretation reads as follows: This graph shows the growth of the population of the United States from 1790 to 1980 and estimates growth to 2050. The horizontal axis represents years in fifty-year intervals. The vertical axis represents the population in units of 100

Figure 1 Growth of the population of the United States of America from 1790 to 1980, with an estimate of continued growth to 2050. (Based on figures from the U.S. Bureau of the Census.)

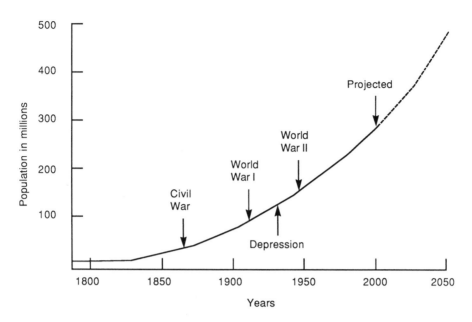

million. The trend revealed by this graph is that the population of the United States began to increase dramatically around 1850 and continued to accelerate through 1980. If this trend holds, the population of the United States will double itself between 1980 and 2050.

Useful Expressions

This graph shows _____.

The subject of this graph is _____.

This format clearly illustrates this subject.

The horizontal axis represents _____.

The vertical axis represents _____.

The line on the graph illustrates the relationship between _____ and _____.

The $\begin{bmatrix} \text{trend} \\ \text{pattern} \end{bmatrix}$ revealed by this graph is _____.

One of the $\begin{bmatrix} \text{trends} \\ \text{patterns} \end{bmatrix}$ that becomes clear from this graph is _____.

If this trend holds _____.

(*Continued*)

By studying this graph, we can predict that _____.

What are some of the implications evident from studying this graph?
    One is _____. Another is _____.

In conclusion, _____.

Assignment 1: Interpreting Graphs

Your teacher will divide the class into pairs. Prepare an interpretation of one of the graphs in Figures 2 through 5 using Worksheet 1. You may wish to refer back to the sample interpretation on pages 13–14. Take turns explaining the graph to each other using the notes you made on the worksheet.

Figure 2   Pull to the South and West, indicated by graphing the share of the population by region. Note: Figures may not add, due to rounding. (Adapted from *U.S. News & World Report*. Basic data from U.S. Department of Commerce.)

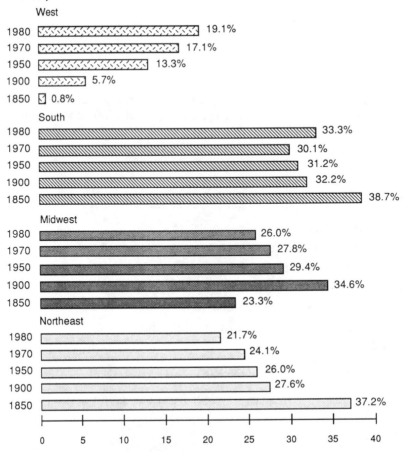

Figure 3 World consumption of primary nonrenewable (shaded) and renewable (nonshaded) energy by source in 1983 with projections for 2000. (From U.S. Department of Energy and Worldwatch Institute.)

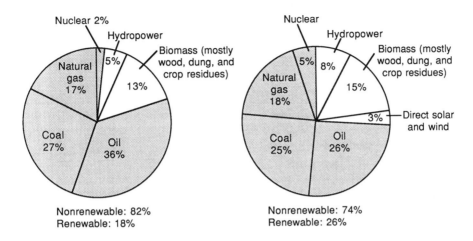

Nonrenewable: 82%
Renewable: 18%

Nonrenewable: 74%
Renewable: 26%

Figure 4 The budget dollar of the United States government. (From U.S. Bureau of the Census, *Statistical Abstract of the United States: 1968,* 89th ed. [1968], p. 377.)

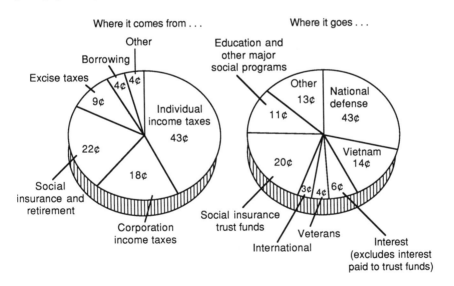

Figure 5 How marriage makes women earn less—and men more. This information is based on all races, aged twenty-five to sixty-four, using median annual incomes for 1984. (From U.S. Bureau of Census, *Current Population Report,* series P60, #151, Table 31.)

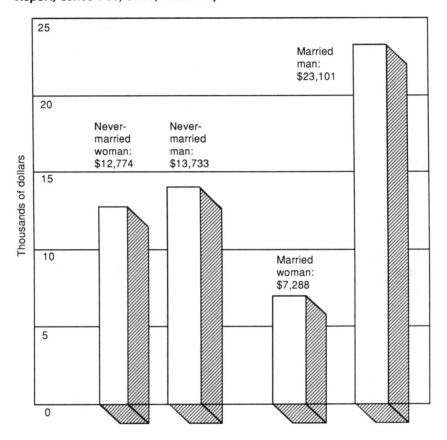

Tables

What Is a Table?

A table is a list that presents numerical data in columns. The data are usually arranged in either descending or ascending order.

How Do You Interpret a Table?

To understand a table you must answer the following questions:

1. What is the subject of the table?

2. What are the headings for each column?

3. What order are the data presented in?

4. What conclusions can you draw from the table?

The following is an example of how to interpret a table (Table 1).

**Table 1/Ethnic Background of 3.7 Million Asians
and Pacific Islanders Living in the U.S., 1980 Census**

Chinese	812,178
Filipino	781,894
Japanese	716,331
Asian-Indian	387,223
Korean	357,393
Pacific Islander	259,566
Vietnamese	245,025
Laotian	47,683
Thai	45,279
Cambodian	16,044
Pakistani	15,792
Indonesian	9,618
Hmong	5,204
Others	26,757

Note: Does not include 380,500 refugees from Vietnam, Laos, and Cambodia who came to the U.S. after the 1980 census.

1. *Subject of the table:*
   This table shows the breakdown of Asians and Pacific Islanders in the United States in 1980.

2. *Presentation order of the data:*
   The data are presented in descending order, with the highest number listed at the top of the column and the lowest number listed last, at the bottom of the column.

3. *Heading for each column:*
   The left-hand column indicates the ethnic background of the Asians and Pacific Islanders who lived in the United States at the time of the 1980 census. The right-hand column indicates the number of people in each ethnic group.

4. *Conclusion(s):*
   Although the 3.7 million Asians and Pacific Islanders living in the United States in 1980 represent over thirteen different ethnic groups, three groups (Chinese, Filipino, and Japanese) account for almost two-thirds of the total.

The complete interpretation reads as follows:
This table shows the breakdown of Asians and Pacific Islanders in the United States in 1980. The data are presented in descending order, with the highest number listed at the top of the column and the lowest number listed last, at the bottom of the column. The left-hand column indicates the ethnic background, and the right-hand column indicates the number of people in each ethnic group. One conclusion that can be drawn from the table is that, although the 3.7 million Asians and Pacific Islanders living in the United States in 1980 represent over thirteen different ethnic groups, three groups (Chinese, Filipino, and Japanese) account for almost two-thirds of the total.

Useful Expressions

This table shows _____.

The subject of this table is _____.

The data are presented in ascending order, with the lowest number listed at the top of the column and the highest number listed last, at the bottom of the column.

The data are presented in descending order, with the highest number listed at the top of the column and the lowest number listed last, at the bottom of the column.

The left-hand column indicates _____.

The right-hand column indicates _____.

The column on the left represents _____.

The column on the right represents _____.

The columns on the table illustrate the relationship between _____ and _____.

One of the $\begin{bmatrix} \text{trends} \\ \text{patterns} \end{bmatrix}$ that become clear from this graph is _____.

By studying this table, we can predict that _____.

One of the implications evident from studying this table is _____. Another is _____.

In conclusion, _____.

Assignment 2: Interpreting Tables

In pairs, prepare an interpretation of one of the tables (Tables 2, 3, and 4) using Worksheet 2. Take turns explaining the table to each other using the notes you made on the worksheet.

Table 2/Occupational Distribution of Employed Women, March 1985

Percent female in various occupations

All occupations	44%
Mechanics	3%
Transportation workers	9%
Farmers, fishers, forestry	16%
Laborers	17%
Craft and kindred workers	21%
Nonretail sales	32%
Managers and administrators	35%
Machine operators	41%
Professionals (except teachers)	41%
Service (except private household)	63%
Retail sales	69%
Teachers (except college)	73%
Clerical	84%
Private household	97%

Source: U.S. Department of Labor, 1985.

Table 3/How City Populations Changed from 1980 to 1982

	Latest estimate	2-year change
New York	7,086,096	+0.2%
Los Angeles	3,022,247	+1.8%
Chicago	2,997,155	−0.3%
Houston	1,725,617	+8.2%
Philadelphia	1,665,382	−1.4%
Detroit	1,138,717	−5.3%
Dallas	943,848	+4.3%
San Diego	915,956	+4.6%
Phoenix	824,230	+4.3%
San Antonio	819.021	+4.2%
Honolulu	781,899	+2.5%
Baltimore	774,113	−1.6%
Indianapolis	707,655	+1.0%
San Francisco	691,637	+1.9%
San Jose	659,181	+4.7%
Memphis	645,760	−0.1%
Washington	633,425	−0.8%
Milwaukee	631,509	−0.8%
Columbus	570,588	+1.0%
New Orleans	564,561	+1.2%
Boston	560,847	−0.4%
Cleveland	558,869	−2.6%
Jacksonville	556,370	+2.9%
Denver	505,563	+2.6%
Seattle	490,077	−0.8%

Source: U.S. News & World Report, April 16, 1900.

Table 4/What It Costs in Cities Abroad

The U.N. calculated how much its officials need for lodging and meals, including tips, when they travel on U.N. business and exchange U.S. dollars at tourist rates. Here's how much the survey found is required per day.

Kinshasa, Zaire	$190
Jidda, Saudi Arabia	$163
New York City	$138
Beirut, Lebanon	$127
Hong Kong	$125
Lagos, Nigeria	$124
London, England	$115
Seoul, South Korea	$110
Tokyo, Japan	$108
Cairo, Egypt	$107
Jakarta, Indonesia	$ 95
Bangkok, Thailand	$ 88
Damascus, Syria	$ 85
Lima, Peru	$ 82
Teheran, Iran	$ 81
Havana, Cuba	$ 76
Toronto, Canada	$ 74
Rome, Italy	$ 64
Bombay, India	$ 63
Manila, Philippines	$ 62
Paris, France	$ 60
Peking, China	$ 58
Rio de Janeiro, Brazil	$ 50
Mexico City, Mexico	$ 50
Buenos Aires, Argentina	$ 48
Rangoon, Burma	$ 47
Quito, Ecuador	$ 43
Athens, Greece	$ 43
Luang Prabang, Laos	$ 27

Assignment 3: Writing and Presenting Graphs and Tables

In this assignment you will have an opportunity to gather data and organize them into an original graph or table. The subject of your graph or table will be drawn from information gathered about your class.

Preparation

1. Your teacher will divide the class into pairs.

2. Gather data from the entire class on one of the topics below:
   a. What are the ages of the students in your class (18–20, 21–25, 26–30, and so on)?
   b. Which countries are represented?
   c. What are the students in your class majoring in?
   d. Do the students in your class come from large or small cities (under 10,000; 10,000–20,000; 20,000–50,000, and so on)?
   e. What religions are represented in your class?
   f. How many different languages are represented in your class?
   g. How long have your classmates studied English?

3. Organize your data into an appropriate graph or table.

4. Your teacher will collect all of the original graphs and tables and redistribute them so that each pair has a graph or table that was constructed by another pair of students in the class.

Presentation

In this activity, you and your partner will interpret a graph or table for the entire class.

1. Prepare an interpretation of the graph or table using Worksheet 3 or Worksheet 4. Take turns explaining it to each other using your notes. Be sure your presentation is equally divided between you and your partner.

2. When it is time for you and your partner to give your presentation, both of you will go to the front of the class. Each of you will present your section in turn.

3. Answer any questions your classmates may ask.

Worksheet 1/Interpreting a Graph

Name _____

Date _____

Use this worksheet to prepare your interpretation of your graph. You may wish to refer back to the sample interpretation on pages 16–17.

1. What is the subject of the graph?

2. What do the horizontal and vertical axes represent?
   Horizontal axis

   Vertical axis

3. What trend or pattern does the graph reveal?

4. What are the implications of the graph? What predictions can you make, or what conclusions can you draw?

Write out your complete interpretation in the space on the next page.

Worksheet 2/Interpreting a Table

Name

Date

Use this worksheet to prepare your interpretation of your table. You may wish to refer back to the sample interpretation on pages 21–22.

1. What is the subject of the table?

2. What are the headings for each column?

3. What order are the data presented in?

4. What conclusions can you draw from the table?

Write out your complete interpretation in the space on the next page.

Worksheet 3/Interpreting an Original Graph

Name _____

Date _____

1. What is the subject of the graph?

2. What do the horizontal and vertical axes represent?
   Horizontal axis

   Vertical axis

3. What trend or pattern does the graph reveal?

4. What are the implications of the graph? What predictions can you make, or what conclusions can you draw?

Write out your complete interpretation in the space on the next page.

Worksheet 4/Interpreting
an Original Table

Name

Date

1. What is the subject of the table?

2. What are the headings for each column?

3. What order are the data presented in?

4. What conclusions can you draw from the table?

Write out your complete interpretation in the space on the next page.

CHAPTER 3

Defining Terms

Skills used in this chapter:
—defining terms
—checking comprehension
—answering questions
—discussing information
—reporting information
—adjusting presentation to level of audience

In this chapter you will learn to present clear and complete definitions of important terms and concepts. You will also learn and practice a more sophisticated and extended type of definition called an *analogy*, which is often used in academia to explain and illustrate difficult or unfamiliar concepts through comparison.

Why Practice Defining Terms?

In academia, clear definitions of important concepts are essential in both oral and written work. Failure to precisely define terms can result in miscommunication and confusion.

Why Is the Analogy Included in a Chapter on Defining Terms?

An analogy is a particular type of definition that explains or illustrates by giving a point-by-point comparison of two different things. It is especially useful when defining terms that are either abstract or completely unfamiliar to your listeners. For example, you might explain to a layman how a computer functions by comparing it to the functioning of the human brain. Additional examples may be found in the section of this chapter dealing specifically with the analogy (see pp. 40–43).

Assignment Overview

You will work with a partner on all of the activities in this chapter. You will begin by defining a term. Next, you will analyze two analogies. Finally, you will develop an original analogy, which either you or your partner will present to the class.

Basic Definitions

What Should You Include in Your Definition?

Before you prepare a definition, you need to ask yourself five basic questions:

1. Why does my audience need to know the definition of this term?

2. How much does my audience already know about this term and about the subject in general?

3. What related ideas and concepts does my audience already know that I can incorporate in my definition to help them understand this unfamiliar term?

4. What does the term mean?

5. What familiar concrete examples will help my audience understand this new term?

The following is an example of how to construct a definition using these five questions. Follow along as your teacher goes through the steps in the example. Useful phrases that you will want to use in your own definitions have been underlined, so please pay special attention to how these phrases are used. After the step-by-step definition is the entire definition as it might be given in an academic presentation.

Example: Preparing a definition of *affective domain,* as it might appear in a talk on second language acquisition

Step 1: Why does my audience need to know the definiton of this term?

This term is basic to any discussion of personality. It has been useful in discussing the personality variables that we observe in second language learners.

Step 2: How much does my audience already know about this term and about the subject in general?

The audience has no familiarity with the term and very little familiarity with the subject of second language acquisition.

Step 3: What related ideas and concepts does my audience already know that I can incorporate in my definition to help them understand this unfamiliar term?

Affective domain is a technical term for the feelings and emotions that everyone experiences. It is often contrasted with the cognitive domain, which refers to our rational and analytical abilities and to our memory.

Step 4: What is the definition?

The affective domain refers to the emotional side of human behavior. This is contrasted with the cognitive side of human behavior, which deals with learning, analyzing, and remembering.

Step 5: What familiar concrete examples will help my audience understand this new term?

An example of a personality factor that falls within the affective domain is the idea of self-esteem or self-confidence. Your self-esteem has to do with your view of yourself. In terms of second language acquisition, we often assume that high self-esteem leads to success in language acquisition. Another personality factor that falls within the affective domain is motivation. Lack of motivation or a lack of desire to learn another language can hinder a person's progress.

The following is the completed definition of the term *affective domain.*

Before I proceed with my talk on second language acquisition, I need to define an important concept, *affective domain*. This term is basic to any discussion of personality. It has been useful in discussing the personality variables that we observe in second language learners. Affective domain refers to the feelings and emotions that everyone experiences. It is often contrasted with the cognitive domain, which refers to our rational and analytical abilities. The affective domain refers to the emotional side of human behavior. This is contrasted with the cognitive side of human behavior, which deals with learning, analyzing, and remembering. An example of a personality factor that falls within the affective domain is the idea of self-esteem or self-confidence. Your self-esteem has to do with your view of yourself. In terms of second language acquisition, we often assume that high self-esteem leads to success in language acquisition. Another personality factor that falls within the affective domain is motivation. Lack of motivation or a lack of desire to learn another language can hinder a person's progress.

Useful Expressions

It is important that you understand what _____ $\begin{bmatrix} \text{means} \\ \text{is} \end{bmatrix}$
   because you will need to _____.

In order to understand the material that we will cover today, we need to
   define the term _____.

One interesting aspect of this topic is _____.

I will be giving you a $\begin{bmatrix} \text{basic} \\ \text{general} \\ \text{simplified} \end{bmatrix}$ definition. This term may have other
   meanings, but for our purposes, it means _____.

This term is used generally to mean _____.

The term _____ differs from _____ because _____.

A _____ differs from _____ because _____.

The term _____ is similar to _____ in that they both refer to _____.

A _____ is similar to _____ in that both are used to _____.

In the field of _____, the term refers to _____, but in the field of _____,
   the term refers to _____.

_____ means _____.

_____ refers to _____.

By _____, I mean _____.

We will define the term _____ in the following way: _____ means _____.

Let me give an example: _____.

To better understand this, we might, for example, $\begin{bmatrix} \text{look at} \\ \text{compare} \\ \text{examine} \end{bmatrix}$ _____.

This example might help you understand _____.

Assignment 1: Defining a Term

In this assignment, you will prepare a definition and practice it with a partner.

Preparation

1. Choose a term from the list below. These are only suggestions; you may select another term if you wish.

2. Prepare your definition using Worksheet 1.

Biology	*Economics*	*Physics*
symbiosis	gross national product	quark
recombinant DNA	inflation	Doppler effect
mutation	recession	entropy
species	stagflation	relativity

Chemistry	*Philosophy*	*Mathematics*
radioactivity	truth	integer
gas	knowledge	function
oxidation	being	set
electrolysis	aesthetics	algorithm

Psychology	*Sociology*
motivation	peasant
aggression	culture
neurosis	ethnicity
extrovert	religion

Presentation

1. Choose a partner.

2. Present your definition to your partner.

3. After you present your definition, ask questions to make sure your partner understands it.

4. Your partner may wish to make some suggestions to help you improve your definition.

Analogies

Now that you have practiced the basic definition, you are ready to practice a more sophisticated type of definition called the analogy. At the beginning of this chapter, we said that an analogy is an extended illustration that explains or illustrates by giving a point-by-point comparison of two different things. It is like a long definition. The analogy is very useful when you are explaining a concept that is abstract, difficult, or unfamiliar to your audience, because it compares this new concept to something that is very familiar and common. The power of the analogy comes from the fact that, although the two things being compared are quite dissimilar, they do *share* important characteristics. For example, a galaxy and a raisin cake that is baking would seem to have little in common, and yet in one important aspect—movement—they are strikingly similar. It is the *apparent* dissimilarity that gives the analogy its force.

Let's begin our work on the analogy by looking at this example from physics, which illustrates the phenomenon that the different clusters of galaxies are constantly moving apart from each other. Read through the analogy in class with your teacher, and answer the questions that follow.

WHEN TIME BEGAN
Fred Hoyle

Observations indicate that the different clusters of galaxies are constantly moving apart from each other. To illustrate by a homely analogy, think of a raisin cake baking in an oven. Suppose the cake swells uniformly as it cooks, but the raisins themselves remain of the same size. Let each raisin represent a cluster of galaxies, and imagine yourself inside one of them. As the cake swells, you will observe that all the other raisins move away from you. Moreover, the farther away the raisin, the faster it will seem to move. When the cake has swollen to twice its initial dimensions, the distance between all the raisins will have doubled itself—two raisins that were initially an inch

---

Reprinted from *The Saturday Evening Post*, © 1959. The Curtis Publishing Company.

apart will now be two inches apart; two raisins that were a foot apart will have moved two feet apart. Since the entire action takes place within the same time interval, obviously the more distant raisins must move apart faster than those close at hand. So it happens with the clusters of galaxies.

The analogy brings out another important point. No matter which raisin you happen to be inside, the others will always move away from you. Hence the fact that we observe all the other clusters of galaxies to be moving away from us *does not mean that we are situated at the center of the universe.* Indeed, it seems certain that the universe has no center. A cake may be said to have a center only because it has a boundary. We must imagine the cake to extend outward without any boundary, an infinite cake, so to speak, which means that however much cake we care to consider there is always more.

Questions

1. What is the universe compared to?

2. What are clusters of galaxies compared to?

3. What happens as a raisin cake bakes?

4. What phenomenon in physics is this compared to?

Useful Expressions

This analogy compares a _____ and a _____.

A _____ is like a _____ in that they both _____.

Could you go over that again?

Would you mind repeating that?

I'm not sure I'm following you.

Could you give us an example?

Have I expressed it clearly?

Have I explained this clearly?

Are there any questions?

Would anyone like me to repeat something?

Let me rephrase what I just said.

Let me put it another way.

What I meant was _____.

Let me give you an example.

Assignment 2: Analyzing Analogies

The purpose of this assignment is to familiarize you with the structure of the analogy. This should make it easier for you to prepare and present an original analogy.

1. Your teacher will divide the class into pairs.

2. Read the passages entitled "Are Social Scientists Backward?" and "Silent Spring."

3. Analyze each analogy by answering the questions that follow each passage.

4. Your teacher will go over each analogy and the questions in class.

ARE SOCIAL SCIENTISTS BACKWARD?
Donald L. Kenmerer

In discussing the relative difficulties of analysis which the exact and inexact sciences face, let me begin with an analogy. Would you agree that swimmers are less skillful athletes than runners because swimmers do not move as fast as runners? You probably would not. You would quickly point out that water offers greater resistance to swimmers than the air and ground do to runners. Agreed, that is just the point. In seeking to solve their problems, the social scientists encounter greater resistance than the physical scientists. By that I do not mean to belittle the great accomplishments of physical scientists who have been able, for example, to determine the structure of the atom without seeing it. That is a tremendous achievement; yet in many ways it is not so difficult as what the social scientists are expected to do. The conditions under which the social scientists must work would drive a physical scientist frantic. Here are five of those conditions. He can make few experiments; he cannot measure the results accurately; he cannot control the conditions surrounding the experiments; he is often expected to get quick results with slow-acting economic forces; and he must work with people, not with inanimate objects.

Quoted in Robert Bander, *American English Rhetoric*, Third Edition (New York: CBS College Publishing, 1983, p. 139).

Questions

1. Which type of athlete is the physical scientist compared to?

2. Which type of athlete is the social scientist compared to?

3. Although scientists and athletes appear to be quite different, what common characteristic does the author point out?

4. Both the swimmer and the social scientist encounter resistance. What is the source of resistance for each?

FROM *SILENT SPRING*
Rachel Carson

In Greek mythology the sorceress Medea, enraged at being supplanted by a rival for the affections of her husband Jason, presented the new bride with a robe possessing magic properties. The wearer of the robe immediately suffered a violent death. This death-by-indirection now finds its counterpart in what are known as "systemic insecticides." These are chemicals with extraordinary properties which are used to convert plants or animals into a sort of Medea's robe by making them actually poisonous. This is done with the purpose of killing insects that may come in contact with them, especially by sucking their juices or blood.

Questions

1. What two things are being compared?

2. What are the shared characteristics?

Assignment 3: Developing an Original Analogy

Your teacher will divide your class into pairs. Working with your partner, you will develop an analogy and practice it; then one of you will be chosen by the teacher to present it to the class. Use Worksheet 2 to prepare your analogy.

Preparation: Guidelines for preparing an analogy

1. Choose a term or concept that can easily be developed into an analogy.

2. Choose a concept from everyday life that is apparently dissimilar to your concept but that shares some fundamental characteristics with the concept you chose above. You now have the raw materials for your analogy.

3. Develop a point-by-point comparison of these two concepts by listing their points of similarity.

Practice

1. Present your analogy to your partner. As you are giving your analogy, ask questions to make sure that your partner understands what you are saying.

2. Your partner will make suggestions on how you can improve your analogy.

3. Revise your analogy according to your partner's suggestions.

Presentation

1. One member of each pair will present the analogy to the class.

2. After the presentation, the speaker will ask an audience member to restate the analogy. This is one of the best ways to ensure that the audience has understood your meaning.

3. If the audience member has difficulty restating the analogy, the speaker should clarify the points of confusion.

Worksheet 1/Definition

Name _____

Date _____

Choose your term and prepare a definition guided by the questions below. Be sure to use the expressions you practiced in Assignment 1.

Term: _____

1. Why does my audience need to know the definition of this term?

2. How much does my audience already know about *this term* and about *the subject* in general?

3. What related ideas and concepts does my audience already know that I can incorporate in my definition to help them understand this unfamiliar term?

4. What does the term mean?

5. What familiar concrete examples will help my audience understand this new term?

   a.

   b.

   c.

Write out your complete definition in the space below.

Worksheet 2/Analogy

Name _____

Date _____

Use this worksheet to prepare your original analogy.

1. Choose a term or concept that can easily be developed into an analogy.

   _____

2. Choose a familiar concept that is in many ways different but that shares some fundamental characteristics with the concept you choose above.

   _____

3. List the points of similarity.

   a. _____

   b. _____

   c. _____

   d. _____

Remember:

1. An analogy is a type of definition. The goal is not merely to list the similarities between things but to define a term or concept.

2. Be sure to use the Useful Expressions on page 41 when you give your analogy. You may refer to this worksheet while giving your presentation.

(Over)

Write out your complete analogy in the space below.

UNIT TWO

Discussing Information

CHAPTER 4

Discussing an Article

Skills used in this chapter:
— gathering information
— defining terms
— discussing information
— asking questions
— answering questions
— leading a discussion
— taking notes

This chapter introduces the unit entitled Discussing Information. The focus of the activities is on learning to participate in and to lead both small group and large group discussions. The basis for these discussions is an article entitled "In Short, Why Did the Class Fail?" by Henry Ottinger, a college writing instructor. It has been placed at the end of this chapter for easy reference.

Why Discuss an Article?

Readings are the stimuli for almost every authentic academic situation. For this reason, it is crucial that you be able to master a given text and discuss its content, style, and implications, as well as respond with your own ideas to the information and opinions presented by the author.

Why Discuss This Article in Particular?

We've chosen this article for two reasons. First, it introduces many issues that are important in American education, such as the responsibilities of the teacher and of the student, the goal of education, and the purpose of college. Now that you are studying in the United States, it is important for you to become familiar with these issues. Second, since students are interested in the topic of education and have strong opinions about it, we hope the article will stimulate the free exchange of these opinions.

How Should You Approach This Article?

It is important to understand from the beginning that this article is the written version of a talk that a writing instructor, Henry Ottinger, gave to his undergraduate writing students at the end of the semester. The article states the particular point of view that a particular teacher presented to a particular class of students at a particular point in time. Because it is so personal and so specific, you may not agree with many of the things that he says. That is fine. The purpose is *not* to persuade you to accept Ottinger's opinions or to say that his opinions are representative of American education. The purpose *is* to help you sharpen your own opinions about certain issues and values in education.

Assignment Overview

Before you actually participate in a discussion of this article, you will do several preparatory activities.

1. You will listen to the article given as a lecture.
2. You will define some of the new terms found in the article and answer questions about the content of the article.
3. You will participate in a class discussion on the information and opinions presented by the author.

After these preparations, you will take part in a small group discussion in which you and your classmates can exchange your own opinions about the issues raised in the article.

I'm working on an assignment for my English class, and I'd like to know if you could help me.

I need your help defining some expressions from an article I'm reading.

    The first term is _____.

    What does it mean in this sentence?

    Does it have a good connotation or a bad connotation?

    I don't quite understand you—could you give me another example?

    Could you repeat that please?

    Let me try to explain it back to you.

    Did you say that _____ means _____?

    Thank you very much for helping me.

    Thank you very much for your time.

I think _____.

I believe _____.

I strongly believe _____.

In my opinion _____.

I personally think _____.

As I see it _____.

Yes, but don't you think _____?

I agree with you, but _____.

Yet on the other hand _____.

But don't forget _____.

For example, _____.

I have several examples that will illustrate my point.

Since this article was originally given as lecture to a class, before reading it, you will hear it spoken by your teacher as if your teacher were addressing these remarks to your class. Pay particular attention to your teacher's tone of voice and to the attitude toward the class that the tone conveys. Does your teacher sound concerned? Sarcastic? Caring? Disgusted? Responsible?

Assignment 1: Defining Terms

Now that you have heard the article given as a lecture, read it carefully several times. The article is written in an informal style, with many new idioms and words. In order to understand the article, you must know the meaning of these words and phrases. Because of the informal sense of these expressions, they cannot simply be looked up in the dictionary. Rather, you must depend on a native speaker's explanations.

1. Your teacher will divide you into groups of three or four and appoint a group leader.

2. The group leader will divide the thirty-six new terms in the article equally among all members of the group (including the leader).

3. You are responsible for getting the definitions of your terms from a native speaker and explaining them to the other members of the group. Ask one of your American friends to explain the meaning of each of your terms. Be sure to show your friend the article so that the context in which each of the terms is used is clear. Write down your friend's explanation of each of the terms.

Assignment 2: Discussing the New Terms and Phrases

1. Assemble in your groups with your completed definitions.

2. Take turns explaining your terms to your group.

3. Be prepared to answer any questions from your group.

4. Use Worksheet 1 to take notes on your classmates' definitions.

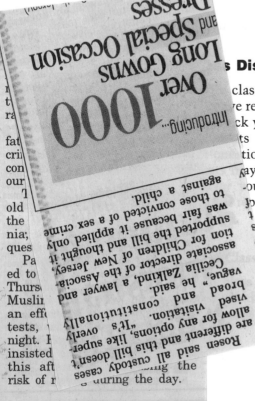

s Discussion?

class participates in a discussion of an
e read. In most discussions of this type,
ck your understanding of the article. In
ts to take an active role in class by
tions. Some of the questions may be
ay contribute to a single answer. For
ou to listen carefully to what your
peat what others have said or miss an

Discussion

scussion based on an article, all
article carefully so that they can
ely without constantly referring

back to the article. The following ten questions cover the content of the article "In Short, Why Did the Class Fail?" At home, study the article and write out a short answer to each of the questions.

Questions for class discussion

1. Explain in your own words the quote from *The Student as Nigger*. According to Farber, how do schools teach? Why is the way they teach harmful?

2. Based on Farber's views, what method or approach did Ottinger use? How did he organize the class? (See paragraph 3.)

3. Was his method successful? (See paragraph 4.)

4. What does Ottinger think of most of the students in the class? Did they "get it together" or "work together"? Did they communicate well with one another? (See paragraphs 6 and 7.)

5. What opportunities did the students have? Did the students take advantage of these opportunities? (See paragraphs 8 to 12.)

6. Does Ottinger believe it is possible for humans to break their conditioning? (See paragraph 14.)

7. Ottinger says that it was to the class's advantage not to break out of the mold. Why was it not to their advantage to do so? Why does he call the students "good little utilitarians"? What does he say are the advantages and disadvantages of "instant things"?

8. How does Ottinger respond to the following remarks: "Gosh, college is no fun"; "It doesn't turn me on"? What does Ottinger believe the goal of education is? (See paragraph 18.)

9. Ottinger concedes that part of the blame lies with the university. What is one solution he recommends for that problem? (See paragraph 19.)

10. Does Ottinger believe that he has failed with all of the students? (See paragraphs 5, 9, and 21.)

Assignment 4: Class Discussion

This activity has several purposes:

1. It gives you practice in formulating answers to content questions based on a reading.

2. It gives you practice in asking and answering questions in front of a group.

3. It prepares you for the next assignment, which is a smaller group discussion.

The work that you did in Assignment 3 will form the basis of the class discussion of the article. The discussion of each question will be led by a different student, appointed by the teacher.

Guidelines for the Class Discussion Leader

1. Read the question aloud to the class.

2. Wait for one of your classmates to volunteer, or call on one or more of them to answer.

3. As leader, it is your responsibility to be sure that the answers are accurate and complete. Use your notes to decide when the question has been answered satisfactorily.

4. When all ten questions have been answered, your teacher will make some general comments to both the leaders and those who answered.

Small Group Discussion

What Happens in a Small Group Discussion?

In a small group discussion, four or five group members explore several viewpoints on a particular subject. In addition to participating in the discussion, one of the group members serves as the group leader, and another member takes notes on the discussion and summarizes the discussion for the entire group.

Why Is It Important to Practice the Small Group Discussion?

In many American universities, students are asked to participate in discussion groups. The groups meet to review lecture notes, to discuss homework, and to work on class assignments and projects.

Guidelines for the Group Discussion Leader

The leader bears much of the responsibility for the success of a small group discussion. It is the leader's job to see that all the members participate, that each member has a chance to fully develop his views, that the discussion does not wander from the topic, and that an accurate record of the discussion is kept.

The leader should do the following:

1. Read the question out loud to the group.
   a. Be sure that all the members understand the question.
   b. Provide background information if it is necessary.
2. Guide the discussion.
   a. Let the other members of the group do most of the talking.
   b. Be sure every member has an opportunity to speak without interruption.
   c. Encourage group members to support their opinions with examples from their own experiences.
   d. Be sure the members listen attentively to one another.
   e. Don't let the discussion wander from the topic.
   f. If there is disagreement, make sure it is expressed in a polite and respectful manner.
3. Appoint someone to take notes on the discussion.

Guidelines for the Note-Taker

1. Take accurate notes on the discussion.
2. Read your notes out loud to the group at the end of the discussion and make the necessary corrections.
3. Present your summary of the discussion to the entire class.

Guidelines for Group Members

A small group discussion cannot succeed without the cooperation and participation of every member. The appropriate behavior for a group discussion member in the United States is listed below:

1. Do not speak until the leader has recognized you.
2. Do not interrupt another speaker.
3. Support your ideas with information from your own experience.
4. Listen carefully to what the other group members say.
5. Be sure that what you have to say is directly related to the topic.

Assignment 5: Small Group Discussion

This assignment builds on the information you learned in assignments 1 to 4 and gives you the opportunity to express your own opinions on some of the important issues raised in the article.

1. Your teacher will divide you into groups of four or five, appoint a group leader, and assign one of the discussion topics.

2. Remember—the leader should:

   a. Read the discussion topic to the group.

   b. Guide the discussion.

   c. Appoint someone to take notes on the discussion.

3. Each group will present its findings to the class and respond to questions and comments.

Topics

1. What is Ottinger's attitude toward his students? What does he mean when he quotes Theodore Roethke: "I love you for what you might be; I'm deeply disturbed by what you are?" What different emotions can you detect in his remarks: anger, sarcasm, affection, discouragement?

2. In your opinion, who was responsible for the failure of Ottinger's class? Was his teaching method reasonable? Were his expectations reasonable? Were the students given too much responsibility? Should the students accept all of the blame for not taking advantage of the opportunities Ottinger listed in paragraphs 8 to 12?

3. Ottinger states several goals of education. What are they? (See paragraphs 10 and 18). Explain and expand the following ideas:

   a. Finding out something about yourselves is the crux of education.

   b. Knowledge for its own sake is a valid and valuable goal.

   c. Real education must ultimately be limited to people who insist on knowing.

4. Ottinger quotes a line from the novel *1984*, by George Orwell: "Freedom Is Slavery." What does that line mean? In what way were the students enslaved by freedom? Did they explore new topics and ideas? Did they use the class to try things they had never done before? Did they fall back on any of their old habits?

IN SHORT, WHY DID THE CLASS FAIL?
Henry F. Ottinger

[1] And now, like it or not, I'd like to say a few [1]parting words.

[2] As you know, I began the semester in a way that departed from the manner in which I had taught composition classes in the past. Much of my attitude at that time was influenced by Jerry Farber's book, *The Student as Nigger*. On the first day of class, I read to you the following:

> School is where you let the dying society [2]put its trip on you. Our schools may seem useful: to make children into doctors, sociologists, engineers— to discover things. But they're poisonous as well. They [3]exploit and enslave students; they [4]petrify society; they make democracy unlikely. And it's not *what* you're taught that does the harm, but *how* you're taught. Our schools teach you by pushing you around, by stealing your [5]will and your sense of power, by making [6]timid, [7]apathetic slaves of you—[8]authority addicts.

[3] That sounded like [9]a breath of fresh air back in February—and I suggested that we try to [10]break the mold, that we could write papers on any subject we wanted, that we could spend class time discussing things—either "the burning issues of the day," or otherwise. You seemed to agree, and we spent a lot of time agreeing together that indeed Farber had the word and we would do what we could to break out of the mold.

[4] As you know, things went from initial [11]ecstasy to final [12]catastrophe. And recently, I fell back—no, you forced me back—into assigning general topics. As a result of that action, and several other factors, this semester has been the worst I've ever taught. In fact, I even debated with myself whether or not to go on teaching next year. But in some ways the semester was valuable because I learned something, if you didn't.

[5] Let me share with you some of the things I learned: and keep in mind that this does not apply to all of you, but it does to the majority.

[6] I learned that all this [13]bull about "getting it together" or "working together" (be it for peace or a grade) is just that—bull. The 1950's were labeled by [14]pop sociologists the "silent generation." I assure you [15]they have nothing on you. Ten years ago, the people around the fountains wore saddle shoes and chinos, and had crewcuts. Now they're barefoot, wear [16]Army fatigues, and have long hair. Big revelation: it's the same bunch of people.

[7] Generally, this class has been the most silent, [17]reticent, [18]paranoid bunch of people in a group I have ever experienced. If you are indicative of the generation that's supposed to change things, good luck. Change is [19]predicated on, among other things, communication between people, "which in your case," as the poem "Naming of Parts" goes, "you have not got."

[8] You had an opportunity to exchange ideas (which it often turned out, "you have not got,") and you were too embarrassed to do so.

[9] You had an opportunity to find out about each other—you didn't. (Or perhaps you found out some of the same things I did: if so, congratulations: the semester has not been a waste for you.)

[10] You had an opportunity to find out something about yourselves. This, by the way, is the [20]crux of education. And, as far as I can see, you found out very little.

[11] You had an opportunity to explore ideas—on your own—and didn't. Most of the papers [21]hashed over the usual [22]cliché-ridden topics: abortion, the SST, the population explosion. One person went so far as to [23]churn out a masterpiece on the pros and cons of [24]fraternities, a topic that was really hot back around 1956.

[12] Most of all, you had the opportunity to be free—free from the usual [25]absurdities of a composition class where topics are assigned, thesis statements are submitted, and so on. You also had freedom of thought, as long as it was [26]confined to the standards of formal English. You had the opportunity to be free—to be responsible to yourselves—and you succeeded in proving to me and to yourselves that Freedom is Slavery, a line from 1984 which I hope, for the sake of all of us, isn't [27]prophetic.

[13] But you protest! (Oh, how I wished you would): "We're incapable of handling all this freedom at once. You see, Mr. Ottinger, we've been [28]conditioned; we're not used to all this!"

[14] Well, I read that in Farber, too, and it's bull. Rats and dogs are conditioned, and are usually incapable of [29]breaking that conditioning. Human beings *can* break conditioning, if it's to their advantage. But here, it's too good an excuse to say "I'm conditioned." Obviously, then, it's to your advantage not to break out of the mold.

[15] *Why* is it to your advantage not to break the mold? In short, why did the class fail?

[16] It failed because, as Dostoevski's "Underground Man" pointed out, thinking causes pain. And, like good little [30]utilitarians, you want to avoid pain. No, it's much easier to come up with instant [31]aesthetics, instant solutions, instant salvation, instant thoughts. After all, instant things, like breakfasts and TV dinners, are easily digestible—and easily [32]regurgitated—and not terribly nourishing.

[17] One of the more [33]atrocious remarks I've heard this semester is, "Gosh, college is no fun," or, when an idea is presented, "it doesn't [34]turn me on."

[18] If you don't believe that knowledge for its own sake is a valid and valuable goal, then you are in the wrong place, and you'd do much better in a vocational school, studying how to be a plumber or a beautician. And if you don't believe, along with Ezra Pound, that "real education must ultimately be limited to men who INSIST on knowing," you are definitely in the wrong place. You are merely [35]clutter.

[19] Granted, there are problems within the University itself—serious problems—that, despite what you may think, show some sign of possible solution. One step they could take (but probably won't) is to limit enrollment, and keep the forty-five percent of you out who don't belong here, because it's no fun.

[20] Well, it's time, I suppose, to bring this to a halt, and let you go over to [36]the Union, or wherever. Until then, I invite you to listen to the lyrics of the Beatles' "Nowhere Man," and if it fits, take it to heart.

[21] Last, I will bid a good-bye (until the final) and say that if at any time some sly hint, or clue, or (God forbid) a half-truth slipped out of my uncon-

scious and slid out the corner of my mouth and, pardon the expression, "turned one of you on," then we have not failed, you and I.

[22] And, to paraphrase Theodore Roethke: I love you for what you might be; I'm deeply disturbed by what you are.

Worksheet 1/Taking Notes
on Your Group Members' Definitions

Term   *Definition*

1.

2.

3.

4.

5.

6.

7.

8.

9.

10.

CHAPTER 5

Lecture and Discussion Section

Skills used in this chapter:
— taking notes on a lecture
— clarifying information
— asking questions
— answering questions
— discussing information

The purpose of this chapter is to take you through a process that is common to university study. You will listen to a lecture and take notes on it, compare your notes with your classmates' notes for accuracy and completeness, and then discuss, from your notes, the content and implications of the lecture.

Why Practice a Discussion Section?

A common course format in American universities is the large lecture class of over 100 students that meets two or three times a week. Because of the large class size, it is difficult for students to raise questions about the lecture material. Consequently, in such courses students are divided into groups of fifteen to twenty that meet once a week with an instructor.

The purpose of these meetings, called *discussion sections*, is to review the lecture material, highlight the important points, and answer questions. Discussion sections are kept small to give all students an opportunity to ask questions and to participate in discussions on the material.

Assignment Overview

The activities in this chapter focus on clarifying information given in a lecture. First, you will take notes on a lecture given by your teacher. After your teacher has given the lecture, you will compare your notes with those of several of your classmates in a small group discussion. Then your teacher will lead the entire class in a discussion to check the accuracy and completeness of your notes. Finally, you will participate in a discussion on the content and ideas in the lecture.

Useful Expressions

What did you get for _____? I got _____.

I wrote down _____. Did someone get something different?

I didn't get anything for _____. Did anybody get that?

I'm not sure about _____. What do you have?

I didn't understand _____.

Do you understand _____?

What does _____ mean?

Would you repeat that definition?

Could you give another example?

Let me rephrase that.

Assignment 1: Taking Notes on a Lecture

Your teacher will give you a lecture on the subject of multiple intelligences. Worksheet 1 is a partially completed outline of the lecture. As your teacher lectures, you will fill in the missing information on the outline. The points in the outline that have already been filled in can serve as landmarks so that you don't get lost during the lecture.

As you listen to the lecture and complete the outline, keep the following points in mind:

1. Your teacher will deliver the lecture at normal speed, so you may not be able to correctly complete the entire outline at one hearing. Don't worry if you miss some points. Even native speakers will miss parts of a lecture.

2. Write down only the essential information.

3. Abbreviate if possible. For example, you may write the word intelligence as "int," or you may write "logical-mathematic" as "log-math."

4. If you miss a point, forget about it and go on. If you do not move on, you'll just get further behind.

5. Sometimes you will only need to write down one word. For an example of this, refer to the outline under "I. Forms of Intelligence," where line G has only one word. In other places, you may want to write out a short phrase or even an abbreviated sentence. For example, on the outline under "V. Testing/Assessing Children's Intelligences," line B has a short phrase.

You are now ready to take notes on the lecture on multiple intelligences. Use Worksheet 1.

Assignment 2: Comparing Your Notes in a Small Group

Now that you have taken notes on the lecture, the next step is to compare your notes with those of your classmates for accuracy and completeness. The goal of this assignment is for your group to discuss and agree upon as complete an outline as possible. In Assignment 3, you will check the accuracy of your group's outline with your teacher.

1. Your teacher will divide you into groups of four or five and appoint a leader.

2. Guided by your group leader, go through the outline point by point, comparing the information you wrote down with the information your classmates wrote down. Make corrections and additions to your outline.

3. If there are some points on the outline that no group member has filled in, don't be concerned. These points will be clarified during the discussion section that follows in Assignment 3.

Assignment 3: Participating in a Discussion Section

In this assignment, you will participate in a *discussion section* where you will check the accuracy of your group's outline against your teacher's outline. This is to ensure that your outline is both complete and accurate. You will then be ready to discuss the content of the lecture in Assignment 4.

1. Your teacher will lead you in a point-by-point discussion of the outline.

2. Every class member should contribute to the discussion.

3. Be sure to ask any questions that you have about the outline.

4. After the discussion, you may refer to the article "Human Intelligence Isn't What We Think It Is" on pages 70–72 to compare your final outline with the original form of the lecture.

Assignment 4: Mastering the Content of the Lecture

The article on multiple intelligences contains some difficult concepts as well as some new vocabulary. The purpose of this assignment is to make sure that you understand everything in the lecture, especially the information in your outline.

Preparation

1. Your teacher will divide you into six groups, one group for each Roman numeral on the outline. Your teacher will also appoint a leader for each group.

2. Each group is responsible for defining the new terms and explaining the concepts in its section.

3. To help you complete this assignment, you may refer to the article "Human Intelligence Isn't What We Think It Is" on pages 63–65.

Presentation

During the *next* class period, the leader of each group will present a brief explanation of the group's section to the entire class. Every member of the group should participate in answering questions from the class.

Complete Outline

Multiple Intelligences

   I. Forms of Intelligence

      A. Linguistic
      B. Logical-mathematical
      C. Spatial
      D. Bodily-kinesthetic
      E. Musical
      F. Interpersonal (dealing with others)
      G. Intrapersonal (knowledge of self)

(continued on page 69)

Worksheet 1/Lecture Outline

"Multiple Intelligences"

I. Forms of Intelligence
   A. _Linguistic_
   B. Logical-mathematical
   C. _Spatial_
   D. Bodily-kinesthetic
   E. _Musical_
   F. _Interpersonal_
   G. Intrapersonal

II. Relative Importance of Different Types of Intelligence
   A. Hunting society
      1. _extremely good control of your body_ spacial
      2. _know your way around_ Body-kinesthetic
   B. _Japanese society_
      1. Interpersonal

III. Emphases of Different Systems of Education
   A. Apprenticeship system
      1. _bodily_
      2. _spatial_
      3. _interpersonal_
   B. _old-fashioned religious schools_
      1. Linguistic
      2. _interpersonal logical mathematical_
   C. Modern secular schools in U.S.
      1. _Linguistic_
      2. Logical-mathematical
   D. Future schools influenced by computers
      1. _logical mathematical_ programming
      2. Intrapersonal
IV. _The foundation for the theory of multiple intelligences_ Biological foundation of theory
   A. All abilities (do/do not) suffer equally when nervous system is damaged
   B. _injury on left hemisphere damage by stroke or tumor_

(Over)

1. Linguistic ability seriously impaired
2. *Don't affect the musical spatial or interpersonal skills not affected*
C. Lesions on right hemisphere *linguistic*
   1. *leave language ~~capacity~~ intact*
   2. *~~seriously compromise~~ spatial musical or interpersonal abilities affected*

V. Testing/Assessing Children's Intelligences
   A. Get rid of *intelligence* and *aptitude* tests
      1. Measure only two forms of intelligence
      2. *destructive social effects*
         a. Short-term success in school
         b. *Very little success outside of school*
   B. Assess intelligence propensities from an early age
      1. *intelligences are not fixed for many years*
      2. *The earlier a strength is discovered, the more flexibility there is to develop it*
      3. Develop profile through learning environments
         a. How children play with blocks
            (1) *How complex are the structures they make*
            (2) Do they remember them?
            (3) *Can they revise them in various ways?*
         b. *Environment could be equipped with musical materials*
      4. Speak of strengths and weaknesses rather than smart and dumb
      5. *The challenge for education*
         a. *Highly developed bodily intelligence: athlete, dancer*
         b. Spatial: *architecture, engineering, sculpture, or surgeon or painting*

VI. Developing Intelligence
   A. Suzuki method *teaching music*
   B. *The more time and energy invested early in life on a particular intelligence, the more you can buoy it up*

Complete Outline (*continued*)

II. Relative Importance of Different Types of Intelligence—varies over time and from culture to culture

    A. Hunting society

        1. Spatial

        2. Bodily-kinesthetic

    B. Japan

        1. Interpersonal

III. Emphases of Different Systems of Education (blends of intelligence keep shifting)

    A. Apprenticeship system

        1. Bodily

        2. Spatial

        3. Interpersonal

    B. Old-fashioned religious schools

        1. Linguistic

        2. Interpersonal

    C. Modern secular schools in U.S.

        1. Linguistic

        2. Logical-mathematical

    D. Future schools influenced by computers (linguistic not important)

        1. Logical-mathematical—programming

        2. Intrapersonal—individual planning

IV. Biological Foundation of Theory

    A. All abilities do not suffer equally when nervous system is damaged (by stroke or tumor)

    B. Left hemisphere damaged (by stroke or tumor)

        1. Linguistic ability seriously impaired

        2. Musical, spatial, & interpersonal not affected to same extent

    C. Lesions on right hemisphere

        1. Linguistic intact

        2. Spatial, musical, interpersonal affected

V. Testing/Assessing Children's Intelligences

    A. Get rid of IQ and aptitude tests

        1. Measure only two forms of intelligence—linguistic & logical-mathematical

        2. Destructive social effects

            a. Short-term success in school

            b. Don't predict success outside of school

B. Assess intelligence propensities from an early age
   1. Intelligences aren't fixed for many years
   2. Earlier it is identified, more flexibility in development
   3. Develop profile through learning environments
      a. How children play with blocks
         (1) How complex are structures?
         (2) Remember them?
         (3) Revise them?
      b. Musical instruments
   4. Speak of strengths and weaknesses rather than smart and dumb
   5. By 10 or 11 speak of "domains"—the career direction a child with certain propensities is likely to go in
      a. Bodily-kinesthetic: athlete, dancer, surgeon
      b. Spatial: architecture, engineering, sculpture, painting

VI. Developing Intelligence
   A. Suzuki method fosters musical intelligence from an early age
   B. The more time and energy invested early in life in a particular intelligence, the more you improve it

---

HUMAN INTELLIGENCE ISN'T WHAT WE THINK IT IS
Howard Gardner

"People Have Multiple Intelligences"
Intelligence is not an absolute such as height that can be measured simply, largely because people have multiple intelligences rather than one single intelligence.

In all, I have identified seven forms of intelligence. The two that are valued most highly in this society are linguistic and logical-mathematical intelligences. When people think of someone as smart, they are usually referring to those two, because individuals who possess linguistic and logical-mathematical abilities do well on tests that supposedly measure intelligence.

But there are five other kinds of intelligence that are every bit as important: Spatial, musical, bodily-kinesthetic and two forms of personal intelligence—interpersonal, knowing how to deal with others, and intrapersonal, knowledge of self. None of these ought to have a priority over others.

"Shifting Importance" of the Seven Varieties
The relative importance of these seven intelligences has shifted over time and varies from culture to culture. In a hunting society, for example, it is a lot more important to have extremely good control of your body and know your way around than to add or subtract quickly. In Japanese society, interpersonal

---

intelligence—the ability to work well in groups and to arrive at joint decisions—is very important.

Historically, different systems of education have emphasized different blends of intelligence. In the old apprenticeship system, bodily, spatial and interpersonal abilities were valued. In old-fashioned religious schools, the focus was on linguistic and interpersonal abilities. The modern secular school emphasizes the linguistic and logical-mathematical, but in the school of the near future I think that linguistic will become much less crucial. For working with computers, logical-mathematical intelligence will be important for programming, and intrapersonal intelligence will be important for individual planning.

What I'm saying is that while both logical-mathematical and linguistic are important today, it won't always be that way. We need to be sensitive to the fact that blends of intelligences keep shifting so that in the future we don't get locked into a specific blend.

Secrets Unlocked by Biological Research

Research in biology has laid the foundation for the theory of multiple intelligences.

Studies show that when someone suffers damage to the nervous system through a stroke or tumor, all abilities do not break down equally. If you have an injury to areas of the left hemisphere of the brain, you will lose your language ability almost entirely, but that will not affect your musical, spatial or interpersonal skills to the same extent.

Conversely, you can have lesions in your right hemisphere that leave language capacity intact but that seriously compromise spatial, musical or interpersonal abilities. So we have a special capacity for language that is unconnected to our capacity for music or interpersonal skills, and vice versa.

I'm not suggesting that this analysis is the last word. I would like to think of it as the first word in a new way of looking at human abilities. . . .

IQ Tests "Have Destructive Social Effects"

I would like to get rid of intelligence and aptitude tests; they measure only two forms of intelligence and have destructive social effects. These tests have been successful because they serve as a good predictor of how people will do in school in the short run. But how much does doing well in school predict success outside of school? Very little.

Those of us who take a position against IQ tests have the burden of coming up with ways of assessing abilities that are not completely impractical. My notion is something between a report card and a test score.

I would assess intellectual propensities from an early age. I use the word *propensities* because I don't believe intelligences are fixed for many years. The earlier a strength is discovered, the more flexibility there is to develop it. Similarly, if a child has a low propensity, the earlier intervention begins, the easier it is to shore up the child. So early diagnosis is important.

Preschools Where "Children Can Do Exploring"

I would not assess abilities through traditional paper-and-pencil tests. Instead, we need learning environments—preschools—in which children can do a lot of exploring on their own or with help from adults.

All children play with blocks, for example, but what do they do with them? How complex are the structures they make? How well can they remember them? Can they revise them in various ways? All of these questions can be answered by adults observing and playing with the children.

The same environment could be equipped with musical materials, and, again, children could explore on their own and with adults. If we had such environments, with periodic monitoring we could develop very good profiles of a child's propensities. This would give parents and teachers a better way of thinking about children than one or two test scores. Instead of looking at a child and saying, "He's smart" or "He's dumb," people would talk in terms of a child's strengths and weaknesses. It is a much more realistic view.

But no theory is going to tell people what to do once a child's propensities are assessed. That decision would depend on the values of those around the child. Some people would say, "Let's go with the child's strengths for all they are worth." Others would say, "It's very important to be good in language, so even though this kid isn't good in it, we're going to work on it."

"The Challenge for Education"

As children mature, the assessments would continue in a different vein. By the age of 10 or 11, the monitoring would shift to "domains," where you might come up with analyses such as "this person has the talent to be a doctor."

While having a high intelligence in an area doesn't predict exactly what you are going to do, it predicts the direction you are likely to move in. If somebody has a very highly developed bodily intelligence, he or she could become an athlete, dancer or surgeon. If somebody has a highly developed spatial intelligence, he or she might be at home in architecture, engineering, sculpture or painting.

The challenge for the educational community is to figure out profiles of young people and then to help them find roles in which they can use their abilities in a productive way.

Recognizing the Diversity of Our Capabilities

The Suzuki method of teaching music, developed in Japan, shows what can be done to foster a specific intelligence when the effort is undertaken intensively at an early age and a lot of energy is put into it. This method creates an environment that is rich with music; mothers play with the youngsters for 2 hours a day from the time they reach age 2. Within a few years, all participants become decent musicians.

In theory, we could "Suzuki" everything. The more time and energy invested early in life on a particular intelligence, the more you can buoy it up. I am not advocating this approach, merely pointing out the possibilities. But before we can make these kinds of decisions, we have to take a first step—recognizing the diverse intelligences of which human beings are capable.

UNIT THREE

Presenting Information

CHAPTER 6

Process Speech

Skills used in this chapter:

—outlining information

—presenting information

In this chapter, you will be asked to organize and present a talk on a process. Because this is the first chapter in the unit entitled Presenting Information, special attention will be given to the skill of outlining, a method for organizing the ideas and information of a talk.

Why Practice the Process Speech?

Many academic disciplines, most notably the natural and social sciences, study process phenomena. A process phenomenon is a connected sequence of actions or events that leads to a particular result or product. When you describe a process, you explain the important steps that lead up to results as diverse as photosynthesis, recessions, earthquakes, droughts, and the assimilation of immigrants into the larger society. Because of their importance in academia, it is important that you be able to explain processes confidently and clearly to both laymen and professionals.

In the first activity in this chapter, you will choose a process and outline a speech that describes it. Then you will practice giving your speech to a partner, and conclude by giving your speech to the entire class.

Outlining

The outline is the predominant organizational scheme used in virtually every academic medium: textbooks, lectures, reports, presentations, and so on. The outline is a method for organizing ideas and information in writing, and when it is used to organize a talk, it becomes a written record of the oral presentation. The ability to outline will aid you not only in preparing talks and writing papers but also in more efficiently extracting information from texts and lectures.

How Is an Outline for a Talk Prepared?

When preparing your outline, it is important to remember that it is the skeleton, or plan, for your entire talk, showing the main points to be covered and the order in which these points will be covered. Most talks have three sections, so your outline will have the same three sections: (1) an introduction, (2) a body, and (3) a conclusion. Visually, your outline will look like the following example of a skeleton outline.

Title: _____

Introduction: _____

_____

_____

Body

  I. Main point

    A. Supporting data

      1.

      2.

    B. Supporting data

      1.

      2.

  II. Main point

    A. Supporting data

      1.

      2.

    B. Supporting data

      1.

      2.

  III. Main point

    A. Supporting data

      1.

      2.

    B. Supporting data

      1.

      2.

Conclusion: _____

_____

_____

Steps to Follow When Preparing an Outline for a Talk

1. State the specific purpose of your talk.

2. Identify the central idea of your subject.

3. Choose two or three main points and express each one concisely.

4. Support each main point with clear examples, and express each supporting idea concisely.

5. Write your conclusion: restate your central idea and main points.

6. Write your introduction: state your central idea and your specific purpose.

The example below illustrates the six steps to use when preparing an outline. The completed outline is also provided.

Example: Preparation of an outline for a talk on the procedures students should follow if they want to arrange an appointment with a professor

Steps	*Example*
1. State the specific purpose.	This talk will describe procedures for consulting with a professor.
2. Identify the central idea.	Many students need extra help from their professors but never get it because they do not know how to arrange for an appointment.
3. Choose three main points.	I. Plan to see the professor before class begins. II. Plan to see the professor during one of her office hours. III. Plan to see the professor by appointment.

4. Support each main point with details.	I. Plan to see the professor before class begins.
	  A. Get to class five minutes before it begins
	  B. When the professor arrives, speak with her in the front of the room.
	    1. Do not ask to speak with her if she arrives late.
	    2. Do not ask to speak with her the day of an exam.

C. State your request clearly.

D. Be sure not to extend your conversation into the class period.

II. Plan to see the professor during one of her office hours.

A. Find out what your instructor's regular office hours are.

B. Go to her office during these times to make sure you will find her in.

C. When you arrive, knock on her door and wait to be invited to enter.

D. State your request clearly.

E. If other students are waiting to speak with the professor, finish with your business promptly.

III. Plan to see the professor by appointment.

A. Arrange for your appointment by telephone or by asking the professor before class.

B. Arrive for your appointment on time.

C. State your request clearly.

D. Leave at the appropriate time.

5. Write your conclusion.

As you can see, if you know what the procedures are, it is an easy matter to see a professor. You can see her before class, during an office hour, or during a special appointment. So don't be afraid to make such arrangements. Most professors expect students to come by with questions and comments and are eager for them to do so.

6. Write your introduction.

Many students need extra help from their professors but never get it because they do not know how to arrange for an appointment. It is easy if you know how to make these arrangements, and in this talk I will tell you how.

Sample outline: Procedures students should follow when making appointments with professors

Introduction: Many students need extra help from their professors but never get it because they don't know how to arrange for an appointment. It is easy if you know how to make these arrangements, and in this talk I will tell you how. I have three points to discuss: how to see the professor before class, how to see her during office hours, and how to see her by appointment.

Body

I. Plan to see the professor before class begins.
    A. Get to class five minutes before it begins.
    B. When the professor arrives, speak with her in the front of the room.
        1. Do not ask to speak with her if she arrives late.
        2. Do not ask to speak with her the day of an exam.
    C. State your request clearly.
    D. Be sure not to extend your conversation into the class period.

II. Plan to see the professor during one of her office hours.
    A. Find out what your professor's regular office hours are.
    B. Go to her office during these times to make sure you will find her in.
    C. When you arrive, knock on her door and wait to be invited to enter.
    D. State your request clearly.
    E. If other students are waiting to speak with the professor, finish with your business promptly.

III. Plan to see the professor by appointment.
    A. Arrange for your appointment by telephone or by asking the professor before class.
    B. Arrive for your appointment on time.
    C. State your request clearly.
    D. Leave at the appropriate time.

Conclusion: As you can see, if you know what the procedures are, it is an easy matter to see a professor. You can see her before class, during an office hour, or during a special appointment. So don't be afraid to make such arrangements. Most professors expect students to come by with questions and comments and are eager for them to do so.

Characteristics of a Good Speaker

Effective communication depends on both form and content: how you say something is as important as what you say. This is particularly true when you are speaking to a group. To ensure effective communication, your presentation should exemplify the following characteristics.

1. Good organization

2. Preparation

   a. Speak from clear and comprehensive lecture notes.

   b. Practice your presentation.

   c. Do *not* read your presentation.

3. Confidence

   a. Do not begin with an apology for your knowledge or your English. If you lack confidence in yourself, the audience will perceive it and lose confidence in you, too.

   b. Be thoroughly prepared and familiar with your material: preparation creates confidence.

4. Responsiveness

   a. Make eye contact with members of the audience. Don't talk to the back wall, the table, or your notes.

   b. Check to see whether the audience is following you.

5. Clarity

   a. Be sure that the organization of your talk is clear to the audience.

   b. Strive for a smooth transition from one point to the next.

   c. Use the blackboard to illustrate and clarify difficult points.

6. Enthusiasm

   a. When something is important, say it slower and louder.

   b. Try to communicate to the audience your own interest in and enthusiasm for your subject: enthusiasm is contagious!

Useful Expressions

I'm going to tell you how to _____.

There are three main steps in this process.

I will focus on three steps in particular.

The first step is _____.

The second step is _____.

The third step is _____.

I have three points to discuss. They are _____, _____, and _____.

Now we are ready to look at the next step in this process.

Now that you know how to _____, I'm going to tell you how to _____.

The most important thing to remember is _____.

Above all, you need to know _____.

Let me repeat that last statement.

As I have shown, _____.

As we have seen, _____.

I hope that you now have a better understanding of how to _____.

Assignment 1: Preparing the Outline for a Process Speech

In this assignment you will prepare the outline for your talk on a process. Remember that in describing a process you are explaining the sequence of steps that leads to a given result or product.

1. Choose a process that you will explain to the class. Choose a subject that you are familiar with and that will be of interest to others. Some examples of process explanations are how to perform a simple experiment, how to use a particular piece of equipment such as a word processor, or how to make something, such as a special type of food that is characteristic of your country.

2. Prepare an outline of your talk using Worksheet 1. This will probably take you from forty-five minutes to an hour.

3. When you have finished your outline, have your teacher look it over before you go on to the next step.

Assignment 2: Practicing and Presenting a Process Speech

1. Practice your talk with a partner. Use your partner's suggestions to revise your talk before you present it to your classmates. *Do not read* from your outline as you are giving your talk. Think of your notes as a map to guide you through your talk.

2. After practicing your talk, you will present it to the entire class. Your outline notes may be used as a reminder. Remember, *do not read* your outline notes.

3. Your teacher may ask members of the audience to complete the Feedback Form on p. 85 and return their copies to you to help you evaluate your presentation.

Worksheet 1/Outline

After choosing your topic, prepare the outline for your talk using the following six steps:

Title: _____

1. State the specific purpose:

2. Identify the central idea:

3. Choose two or three main points:
   I.

   II.

   III.

4. Support each main point with details:

   I.

   A.

   B.

   II.

   A.

   B.

III.

    A.

    B.

5. Write your conclusion:

6. Write your introduction:

Feedback Form

Name of Speaker _____

Topic _____ Total Time _____

Complete this form for one member of the class. Rate the speaker on each point listed below by using this scale of 1 to 4.

Poor			Excellent
1	2	3	4

I. Introduction

___ The purpose was stated clearly.

___ The central idea was stated clearly.

___ The main points were mentioned.

II. Body

___ The main points and supporting data clarified the central idea.

___ The organization was well-planned and the information was easy to follow.

___ The talk was informative: I learned something from it.

___ The speaker made the subject matter interesting.

III. Conclusion

___ The central idea was restated.

___ The main points were summarized.

IV. Overall (Write your comments in the space provided.)

1. What did you like most about this talk?

2. What is the one thing the speaker could do to make a future talk better?

CHAPTER 7

Impromptu Speech

Skills used in this chapter:
—asking questions
—answering questions
—speaking extemporaneously
—leading a discussion
—responding to audience questions
—stating opinions

This chapter introduces the impromptu speech, a short speech given after only a few minutes of preparation.

Why Practice the Impromptu Speech?

The ability to speak in front of a group with minimal preparation will greatly increase your confidence and will serve you well in a variety of academic settings: class discussions, group discussions, formal presentations, and answering questions.

Assignment Overview

The impromptu speech that you will be giving in this chapter is based on an article entitled "Environmental Ethics." The first assignment is intended to help you master the content of the article. Once that has been accomplished, you will give an impromptu speech on an assigned topic from the article in front of the entire class.

Useful Expressions

I agree with this idea, but _____.

I disagree with this point of view.

For example, _____.

For instance, _____.

To illustrate my point: _____.

I'd like to add that _____.

Not to mention the fact that _____.

Furthermore, _____.

In a case/situation like this/that, _____.

In addition, _____.

And another thing: _____.

Do you really think/believe _____?

Do you mean to say _____?

Don't you think _____?

Can you explain why _____?

I don't understand why _____.

Why do you think _____?

What do you mean by _____?

Assignment 1: Understanding the Article

This assignment will help you master the information in the article "Environmental Ethics" to prepare for the impromptu speech you will give in Assignment 2. A thorough knowledge of the article, particularly the eight basic beliefs listed under "Attitudes toward Nature" and the eight ethical guidelines listed under "Sustainable Earth Ethics" will greatly enhance your confidence when you give your impromptu speech.

1. Read the article carefully.

2. Know all new terms and phrases.

3. Be prepared to answer questions covering the content and vocabulary in a class discussion led by your teacher.

ENVIRONMENTAL ETHICS

Attitudes toward Nature

Many analysts argue that ecological concern will be short-lived and ecological action crippled unless we deal with the attitudes and values that have led to environmental degradation. As E. F. Schumacher said, "Environmental deterioration does not stem from science or technology, or from a lack of information, trained people, or money for research. It stems from the life-style of the modern world, which in turn arises from its basic beliefs or its religion."

The attitude of most industrialized nations toward nature can be expressed as eight basic beliefs:

1. Humans are the source of all value (anthropocentrism).
2. Nature exists only for our use.
3. Our primary purpose is to produce and consume material goods. Success is based on material wealth.
4. Matter and energy resources are unlimited because of human ingenuity in making them available.
5. Production and consumption of goods must rise endlessly because we have a right to an ever increasing material standard of living.
6. We need not adapt ourselves to the natural environment because we can remake it to suit our own needs by means of science and technology.
7. A major function of the state is to help individuals and corporations exploit the environment to increase wealth and power. The most important nation-state is the one that can command and use the largest fraction of the world's resources.
8. The ideal person is the self-made individualist who does his or her own thing and hurts no one.

Although we may not accept these statements, most of us act individually, corporately, and politically as if we did—and this is what counts.

How did we get such attitudes toward nature? Historian Lynn White, Jr., among others, traces the Western ecological crisis to the Judeo-Christian acceptance of the biblical directive to "be fruitful and multiply, fill the earth and subdue it, and have dominion over the fish of the sea and over the birds of the air and over every living thing" (Genesis 1:28). Theologians and other scholars have pointed out that this hypothesis treats the Judeo-Christian tradition as a monolithic structure instead of a rich diversity of beliefs operating in many different ways throughout history. They also point out that the Bible calls for stewardship of nature.*

From *Living in the Environment: An Introduction to Environmental Science*, Fourth Edition, by G. Tyler Miller, Jr. © 1985 by Wadsworth, Inc. Used by permission.

---

*Examples are found in Genesis 2:15; Leviticus 25:2–5; Deuteronomy 8:17, 20:19–20, 22:6; Job 38; Psalms 24:1–6, 65:11–13, 84:3, 148; Isaiah 24:4–6; Malachi 3:11–12; Matthew 6:12, 22–39; Luke 12:16–21, 16:1–2.

Some have suggested that the answer lies in Eastern religions, which emphasize humans *in* nature rather than humans *against* nature. For example, Taoism and Zen Buddhism include the idea of the harmony and unity of humans with nature, and Buddhism fosters reverence for all living creatures and an appreciation of the beauty of nature. But people guided by these and other non-Western religions have also ruined land through overgrazing, soil erosion, and excessive deforestation. Thus, some scholars argue that it is not one's professed religion or philosophy of life that is to blame, but the failure of humans to put their religious or philosophical beliefs into practice. Others argue that all the world's religions and philosophies contain anthropocentric (human-centered) views that can and usually do lead to environmental degradation.

Sustainable Earth Ethics

A number of environmentalists urge that we adopt a sustainable earth or conserver world view based on replacing the eight attitudes toward nature listed earlier with the following ethical guidelines.

1. Humans are not the source of all value.
2. Nature does not exist primarily for human use but for all living species. In the words of Aldo Leopold, each of us is "to be a plain member and citizen of nature."
3. Our primary purposes should be to share and care for all humans and to recognize the right of all species to live without interference or control by humans. Success is based on the degree to which we achieve these goals.
4. Matter and energy resources are finite and must not be wasted. As Arthur Purcell puts it: "A conservation ethic means simply a desire to get the most out of what people use, and a recognition that the wasteful use of precious resources is harmful and detrimental to the quality of everyone's life."
5. Production and consumption of material goods need not increase endlessly—no individual, corporation, or nation has a right to an ever-increasing share of the earth's finite resources. "There is enough for everybody's need but not for anybody's greed" (M. K. Gandhi).
6. As part of nature, humans should work with—not against—nature. In the words of Aldo Leopold, "A thing is right when it tends to preserve the integrity, stability, and beauty of the biotic community. It is wrong when it tends otherwise."
7. Major functions of the state are to supervise long-range planning, to prevent individuals and corporations from exploiting or damaging the environment, and to preserve human freedom and dignity.
8. We can never completely "do our own thing" without exerting some effect now or in the future on other human beings and on other living species. All past, present, and future actions have effects, most of which are unpredictable.

Achieving a Sustainable Earth World View

Achieving a sustainable earth world view is not easy because it goes against many of the things we believe.

Now that you are familiar with the article, you are ready to prepare the impromptu speech.

Guidelines for the Impromptu Speech

Remember that the essence of the impromptu speech is the ability to speak confidently and clearly in front of a group with very little preparation. For this reason, you will have only five minutes to prepare your speech. The following steps are essential for a successful impromptu speech:

1. Read your topic carefully. Be sure you understand it clearly.

2. Decide what your position is on the topic. Do you agree or disagree? Then, express your opinion in the form of a statement. For example: "I agree with the idea that the preservation of the natural environment deserves the cooperation of all nations."

3. Write down some notes to help you plan your speech:
   a. Plan your introduction. The simplest introduction is to restate the topic.
   b. Choose two or three examples to support your opinion.
   c. Conclude by repeating your opinion.

How Long Should You Speak?

You should plan to speak for approximately three minutes.

Assignment 2: Giving the Impromptu Speech

In this assignment, you will give your impromptu speech in front of the entire class. For this impromptu speech, you will be asked to agree or disagree with either one of the eight basic beliefs toward nature held by most industrialized nations or one of the eight ethical guidelines held by conservationists urging a sustainable earth or conserver world view.

Before you begin, read through *all* the steps below. This will ensure that this activity proceeds smoothly.

1. The teacher decides the order of all of the speakers and makes a list.

2. The teacher assigns a topic to the first student, who leaves the room for five minutes to prepare an impromptu speech on Worksheet 1.

3. While the first student is out of the room, the teacher assigns two students to ask a question of the first speaker at the conclusion of the speech.

4. When five minutes are up, the teacher calls the first student back into the classroom. Before he gives his speech, the teacher assigns a new topic to the second student, who then leaves the room to prepare. The teacher then chooses two more students to ask questions.

5. As soon as the second student has left the room, the first student gives his speech. The teacher should make sure that the speech (three minutes) plus the questions and their answers (two minutes) do not exceed five minutes.

6. When five minutes are up, the first speaker sits down, the second speaker is called back into the room, and the third speaker is assigned a topic and leaves the room.

7. This procedure is followed until all students have given an impromptu speech.

Worksheet 1/Impromptu Speech

Use this worksheet to prepare your impromptu speech.

  I. Introduction

     _____

     _____

  II. Statement of Agreement or Disagreement

     _____

     _____

     _____

III. Examples

    A. _____

       _____

    B. _____

       _____

    C. _____

       _____

 IV. Conclusion

     _____

     _____

UNIT FOUR

Presenting and Defending a Position

CHAPTER 8

Panel

Skills used in this chapter:
— presenting information
— asking questions
— responding to audience questions
— brainstorming in a small group
— leading a class discussion
— organizing and leading a group
— introducing panel members

The purpose of this chapter is to introduce you to the concept of a panel. A panel discussion combines the skills of giving a speech with those of asking and answering questions.

What Is a Panel?

A panel usually consists of a group of three or four speakers who are experts on various aspects of a single topic, plus a moderator who introduces the speakers. During a panel, each speaker gives a presentation on her area of expertise within a larger topic to an audience of nonexperts.

At the conclusion of all of the presentations, a lively question-and-answer period between the audience and the panel members is directed by the moderator.

Why Practice a Panel?

The panel is important because it is a format commonly used in academia and business and at professional conferences. More broadly, however, the panel gives you the opportunity to practice making a presentation and to practice asking and answering questions.

Assignment Overview

The topics for this panel are all based on the article "Multiple Intelligences," found in Chapter 5. You may wish to review this article before you proceed further in this chapter. Your teacher will divide the class into panels and assign a topic to each panel. Once you have your topic, your panel will select a leader who will lead a general discussion of the topic and then assign one aspect of the topic to each panelist, who will then prepare a six-minute talk. You will then practice your talks in pairs and make necessary revisions. Next, you will practice introductions, since a panel always begins with introductions. The last assignment is the panel presentation.

Useful Expressions

I am pleased to introduce today's panelists.

We are very pleased/fortunate to have with us today Dr./Mr./Mrs./Ms./Professor _____.

Today we have with us four distinguished experts.

Our (first, second, third, fourth) panelist comes to us from the National Academy of Sciences.

Dr./Mr./Professor _____ is affiliated with the National Academy of Sciences.

She has spent the last _____ years doing research in the area of _____.

During that time she has published numerous articles and books on the topic. For example, _____.

Today she's going to speak to us about her recent research on _____.

The title of her talk is _____.

(Continued)

Please hold your questions and comments until all of the panelists have spoken.

Following the presentations there will be a brief question-and-answer period. Please hold your questions until then.

Topics

For this panel on multiple intelligences, there are four basic topics. The nationalities and majors represented in your class will determine which topics are most appropriate for your class. For each topic, there are several possible ways to compose the panel. These possibilities are listed below each topic. Read through the topics below.

Topic 1

Rank the seven types of intelligence in order of importance in your country and justify your ordering by explaining why each type of intelligence is important, if it is.

Options

1. Members of the panel are all from the *same* country. For this option the panel members divide the seven types of intelligence among themselves. The panel moderator will discuss only one type of intelligence, and the other panel members will each discuss two types.

2. Each member of the panel comes from a *different* country. In this case, panelists will cover all seven types of intelligence for their countries. Panelists should rank-order all seven types but should discuss only the four most important types.

Topic 2

Rank the seven types of intelligence in order of importance for your academic major, and justify your ordering by explaining the relative importance of each type of intelligence.

Options

1. Members of the panel all have the same major. For this option, the panel members divide the seven types of intelligence among themselves. The panel moderator will discuss only one type of intelligence, and the other panelists will each discuss two types.

2. Each member of the panel has a different major. In this case, each panelist will cover all seven types of intelligence, but will discuss only the four most important types.

Topic 3

Rank the seven types of intelligence in order of importance. Choose the four types of intelligence that your culture values most in either women or men.

Options

1. Panelists are all from the same country.
    a. Of the four panelists, two are men and two are women. The men describe the four types of intelligence that their country values most in men, and the women describe the four types of intelligence that their country values most in women.
    b. The panel is made up of two men and two women. For this option, the men describe the four types of intelligence that their country values most in women, and the women describe the four types of intelligence that their country values most in men.
2. Panelists are from different countries.
    a. The panel is made up of four men, who describe the four types of intelligence that men in general value most in women.
    b. The panel is made up of four women, who describe the four types of intelligence that women in general value most in men.

Topic 4

Describe how your country fosters the four types of intelligence that it values most.
    Option: All members of the panel are from the same country, so each panelist will discuss one type of intelligence.

Choosing a Topic and Forming Your Panel

1. Your teacher will choose a topic from the four major topics listed earlier, taking into consideration the majors and nationalities represented in the class and the interests of the students. Your teacher will then select an appropriate option for that topic.

2. Your teacher will now form a panel with four members in accordance with the option selected in Step 1 above.

3. Your teacher will follow this procedure to form all of the panels. Where possible, it is desirable for each panel to be given a different topic or option.

Assignment 1: Preparation

A panel discussion is divided into two sections: presentations and a question-and-answer period. In this assignment you will prepare your presentations for the first section.

Assemble in your groups and follow the steps below to prepare for your panel presentations.

1. Choose a group leader who will guide the discussion during this assignment and who will also serve as moderator during the actual panel.

2. Spend twenty to thirty minutes as a group discussing your specific topic. This type of general, small-group discussion is often called *brainstorming*. At this time, you may wish to review the article or your lecture notes.

3. The group leader will then assign each member, including himself, a portion of the topic. The leader should take into account the interests and capabilities of individual panel members when making his topic assignments.

4. Panel members now prepare their six-minute talks on their topics. This may be done either in class or at home. Remember that an interesting talk is one that includes many specific, relevant examples and draws on personal experience.

Guidelines for the Panel Moderator

1. Introduce all panel members including yourself.

2. Make sure that each speaker stays within the six minutes allotted for each presentation.

3. At the conclusion of the last presentation, invite questions from audience members. It is your job to call on audience members with questions and to decide which panelist(s) will provide answers.

4. Close the panel by announcing the end of the question-and-answer period.

Assignment 2: Practice

1. Pair up with another member of your panel.

2. Give your talk to your partner, and then revise your talk, incorporating your partner's suggestions.

3. Repeat these steps for your partner.

4. Now give the revised version of your talk to your partner. Your partner may still have a few suggestions that you can incorporate into your talk.

Assignment 3: Introductions

The panel begins by having the moderator introduce each panel member. These introductions are necessary for the panel members as well as the audience, since often the panelists will not know each other. The following information is included in the introduction:

1. panel member's title and name

2. affiliation

3. brief background that explains why the panelist is an expert on this topic

4. title of the presentation

Now you are ready to practice introducing each other. Follow the steps below:

1. Pair up with your partner from Assignment 2.

2. Interview your partner to gather the information you will need to make a complete introduction. Use Worksheet 1.

3. Using this information, practice introducing your partner to an imaginary audience.

4. Repeat this procedure for your partner.

Practice I

1. Assemble in your panels.

2. Take turns introducing each other to the rest of the panel.

Practice II

During the actual panel, the moderator will make all of the introductions, beginning with himself. To prepare for this, the moderator should now practice introducing each of the panelists.

Assignment 4: Presentation

Below is the outline for your panel presentation. Each panel should take approximately thirty-five minutes, broken down as follows:

Introductions by the moderator: 2 minutes
Individual presentations: 6 minutes for each panelist
Question-and-answer period: 10 minutes

1. The teacher decides the order of the panels.

2. Panel members sit together at a table facing the audience.

3. The moderator introduces each of the panelists, beginning with himself.

4. Panel members give their talks in the order set by the moderator. The moderator should speak last.

5. The moderator now opens the question-and-answer period.

6. The moderator closes the panel by thanking the panelists and audience members for their participation.

7. At the conclusion of the panel, the teacher may wish to comment on both the presentations and the question-and-answer periods.

Guidelines for Panel Audience Members

1. Listen attentively and respectfully to each speaker.

2. Hold your questions and comments until the question-and-answer period.

3. During the question-and-answer period, wait for the moderator to acknowledge you before asking your question or making your comment. You may address your questions and comments to a specific panelist or to the panel in general.

4. In asking your question or making a comment, remember that you are addressing an expert.

Worksheet 1/Preparing an Introduction

Use this worksheet to write down the information you will need to make a complete introduction of one of the members of your panel.

1. Panel member's title and name:

2. Affiliation:

3. Brief background that explains why the panelist is an expert on this topic:

4. Title of the presentation:

Write out the complete introduction in the space below.

CHAPTER 9

Seminar

Skills used in this chapter:
— presenting information
— defining terms
— leading a discussion
— responding to audience questions
— asking discussion questions

This chapter introduces the seminar, a presentation-and-discussion format that is frequently used in American universities, particularly at the graduate level. In the activities that follow you will participate in two seminars, one of which will be based on a series of short readings on American advertising.

What Is a Seminar?

A seminar is a group of students studying under a professor and exchanging information and ideas through reports and discussions. As you can see from the definition, a seminar is a particular type of group discussion. Each member of the group gives a report on one aspect of the general topic being discussed and is expected to be able to answer questions about that portion of the topic.

What Is the Difference between a Seminar and a Panel?

There are several distinctions that can be made between a seminar and a panel:

1. Seminar participants are normally classmates.

2. There is no audience in a seminar.

3. There is no moderator in a seminar. Each speaker guides the question-and-answer session following his presentation, while the professor functions as an advisor.

Why Practice the Seminar?

The seminar is an important part of a student's university experience in the United States. Most college students will participate in several seminars in their majors, so it is important to understand how a seminar is conducted and what is expected of participants. Since it is usually an advanced-level course, instructors have high expectations of their students' abilities to participate successfully in a seminar. Students are evaluated on both (1) their presentations and (2) their participation in the discussions.

How Is a Seminar Organized?

In many seminars, the students discuss a reading assignment. This can be, for example, a scientific article or a work of literature. Each student is required to read the *entire* selection but is responsible only for reporting to the rest of the class on one section of it. The seminar leader, usually the instructor, makes the report assignments and organizes the order of the presentations. Each student makes a presentation and then leads the class in a short discussion of that portion of the assigned reading.

Assignment Overview

In this chapter, you will participate in two seminars. The first seminar, on education, is a practice seminar and therefore draws on your own experience and opinions rather than on a reading. The second seminar, on television advertising in America, is based on several readings.

Let me first explain _____.

The subject that I intend to discuss is _____.

The first important point is _____.

The second point is _____.

The third point is _____.

To illustrate this point, let's consider _____.

On the one hand, _____.

On the other hand, _____.

Since this is so, _____.

Now let us consider _____.

If this is true, _____.

This is important because _____.

The important results are _____.

Let me repeat this.

In order to start the discussion, I'd like to _____.

Are there any questions?

Would you repeat your question, please?

We have time for just one more question.

Since I'm running out of time, I can only give you a brief answer.

I think I'd better end now; I'm out of time.

That's all we have time for.

Before you begin working on your first seminar, your teacher will discuss the seminar guidelines with the class. Be sure that you are thoroughly familiar with them.

Guidelines for the Seminar

If you are the presenter:

1. Know *your* section of the article. You are not expected to be an expert on the entire article. For your presentation, summarize the major points of your portion of the reading and define the new words and phrases. During your presentation, you may refer to your notes, but do not read your presentation.

2. Relate your particular part of the reading to the whole reading assignment.

3. After your presentation, lead the class in a short discussion of the ideas covered in your section. Ask the audience two questions about your presentation. Ask questions about concepts, points of view, and implications rather than about simple facts.

4. Watch your five-minute time limit.

If you are a seminar participant:

1. Prepare for the seminar by reading the entire assignment. Be familiar with the major ideas in the reading.

2. Listen to each report carefully. Take notes and write down questions you may have.

3. Participate in the group discussion following a report.

Assignment 1: Preparation for the Practice Seminar: "Aspects of Education"

The subject of your first seminar is education. Your teacher will divide the class into groups of six to eight. Each of you then selects your individual topic from the list below. As you prepare your presentation, include ideas from your own experience.

Topics

1. Role of the teacher.

2. Role of the student.

3. Discipline in the classroom.

4. The goal of education: moral or practical?

5. Role of the family in education.

6. Role of the government in education.

7. The levels or phases of education.

8. Train the mind only, or mind, body, and spirit?

9. What is the difference between an educated and an uneducated person?

10. The importance of imitation, repetition, originality, and inventiveness.

11. Should education be for everyone, or only for the very bright students?

Preparation

1. You will have thirty minutes to prepare a three-to-five–minute presentation on your topic using Worksheet 1. Remember that you will be asked questions about your presentation, so you should prepare as thoroughly as possible.

2. When the thirty minutes are up, your teacher will assign you a partner. Give your presentation to your partner. Your partner will ask you questions about your talk that you must answer as completely as possible.

3. Your partner will give you suggestions on how you can improve your presentation.

4. Both partners follow this procedure.

Assignment 2: Giving the Seminar: "Aspects of Education"

Each seminar should consist of no more than eight students, so there may be at least two seminars being held simultaneously in your class. The teacher will determine the order of speakers for each seminar and will also keep the time. Each speaker will have three to five minutes for his presentation, followed by a two-minute question-and-answer period led by the speaker. After the last student concludes his presentation, he will close the seminar by highlighting the important and interesting points brought out in the seminar.

Now that you have completed the practice seminar, you are ready to begin work on a more extensive seminar on advertising in America.

Assignment 3: Seminar Overview: "Television Advertising in America"

1. The teacher will assign you one section of the following article. If two of you are assigned to the same section, each of you should share equally in all parts of the seminar activity.

2. Study the *entire* article so that you are familiar with the major ideas in it. Do this at home in preparation for the next class.

3. Carefully study *your assigned portion* of the article. You must be an expert on it.

Assignment 4: Definitions

1. Choose three terms or phrases from your portion of the article that you think will be unfamiliar to your classmates. Choose terms or phrases that:

a. are essential to the meaning of your section

b. are not highly technical

c. add to your general English vocabulary

2. Prepare brief definitions of each new term or phrase using Worksheet 2. Be sure to explain your definitions in a way that your classmates will understand, and use each term in an original sentence or context that clearly illustrates its meaning.

3. In pairs, give your definitions to your partner, who will make suggestions on how they can be improved. Revise your definitions according to your partner's suggestions.

TELEVISION ADVERTISING IN AMERICA

Television: The Ultimate Advertising Medium

Though radio remains a vital force in advertising, it is generally acknowledged that after World War II television became the dominant American entertainment medium. It was only natural that it should become the dominant advertising medium as well. Network radio no longer attracted the mass audience. Advertisers were among the first to perceive this change, and TV was quickly flooded with commercials. Since the new medium reached a heterogeneous audience, products most likely to benefit from TV exposure were those almost everyone could use: toothpaste, aspirin, soap, and cigarettes.

Television was a new challenge for advertisers, since they could now picture the product as well as describe it. A lesson first learned in radio was doubly applicable to television: In a marketplace flooded with similar products, the form of the ad was at least as important as the content. Cigarette commercials in the mid-1950s, for example, showed scene after scene of lush springtime countryside. A playful couple cavorted flirtatiously while smoking. Clearly the message was that smoking (for whatever unknown reason) is like a springtime experience, embodying all the joys of youth, love, and an ant-free picnic.

In 1952 the sale of radio time still accounted for more than 60 percent of every broadcast advertising dollar, but two years later television surpassed radio with sales that exceeded $500 million. By 1956, the total spent buying network radio time had dropped to $44 million, about a third of what it had been at the beginning of the decade.

As in radio, most network television programs were *sponsored*— conceived, created, and paid for by sponsors and their agencies. In 1959, the public was outraged at having been deceived by those rigged quiz shows and blamed the networks. With some justification all three maintained that they were only conduits, selling time to others who created the shows, but it didn't seem to matter.

Networks quickly realized that they would have to control more carefully the content of programs they aired. Increasingly, new shows were conceived

---

From *Mediamerica*, Third Edition, by Edward Jay Whetmore, © 1985 by Wadsworth, Inc. Used by permission.

and produced by the networks themselves. This led to a decline of the sponsorships of shows and the rise of spot advertising. The spot advertiser does not buy any one show but hundreds of 30- or 60-second spots to be run at specified times.

Save Me a Spot

Spot advertising is the backbone of broadcast advertising. Here's how it works:

1. The ad agency meets with the client and determines media strategies most appropriate for the product.
2. A time buyer employed by the agency meets with a station representative, who may handle dozens of radio and TV stations. Together they try to determine which "buys" will be most effective for the client.
3. The station rep designs a package of buys, specifying stations and air times.

   Sometimes a client will intervene by putting other constraints on the time buyer. Often the station rep will try to stick time buyers with the less than desirable times they are under pressure to sell. Eventually the client's spot, conceived and produced by the agency, appears on the station at the time and date specified.

   What I've just described is a simplified version of what happens at the national or regional level. At the local level, sponsors may deal directly with the station sales people. In very small markets, those sales people may also be on-the-air personalities or perform some other function for the station.

Case in Point: The Great Pet-Food War

I want tuna,
I want liver,
I want chicken,
Please deliver.

The cat that sang this refrain for Meow Mix was supposed to persuade us that our cats would never be happy until we delivered the product to them. This is one of the dozens of pet-food commercials in recent years that have "humanized" pets. But when you stop and think about it, pets aren't human at all. Or are they?

Behind these commercials are thousands of hours of research designed to exploit our feelings about pets and to sell us one particular brand of pet food over another. Most veterinarians agree that pets are color blind and that even the taste of a particular food matters very little. Yet most of us are convinced about the virtues of the pet food we buy. Why?

Pet-food commercials afford the perfect example of the victory of form over content in advertising. In Europe, most animals get along on table scraps, but the American pet must have pet food.

This phenomenon is a fairly recent one. According to an article in *The New Yorker*, until about 1960 there were only a few pet foods on the market. But by 1965, Americans were spending $700 million on their pets, and a scant 15 years later that figure had jumped to over $3.2 *billion*. Virtually all of this can be attributed to advertising. Our pets may be no healthier or happier, yet we believe they *must* have these products.

The advertising agencies have us neatly divided into three camps. There's the "premium" buyer, who buys only the best—brands advertised as "100 percent meat and meat by-products." Then there's the "practical" or "functional" consumer, who buys whatever is cheapest—the cereal products. In the middle is the buyer of the "moist meal" pet foods, packaged in convenient foil pouches but supposedly tasting like they "just came out of the can."

The most celebrated coup in the industry was the triumph of the Alpo campaign of the middle 1960s, which insisted "Your dog *needs* meat." The goal was simple: to convince owners that their dogs *had* to have the premium-priced Alpo brand. In 1970, the Federal Trade Commission intervened. Their tests indicated that pets really didn't *need* meat at all. In fact, all pet foods—canned, moist, and cereal—had long been meeting government regulations requiring certain minimum nutritional content.

The new Alpo cry was: "Your dog *loves* meat!" Alpo, of course, was not the only pet food manufacturer to use slogans. Ralston Purina asserted that its Chuck Wagon was "meaty, juicy, chunky." However, Chuck Wagon did not contain one speck of meat.

What motivates us to spend all this money on our pets? The first response is obvious—we love them. We want them to have a "balanced diet," one that's good for them. We have feelings about our pets that have been successfully exploited by sponsors and their agencies. Besides, who can resist a close-up of a kitten or puppy, or the antics of Morris the "finicky" cat? Pets are so . . . well . . . visual! That's why pet-food commercials work so well on television. Despite healthy budgets for radio and print, TV remains first in the pet-food ad business.

Television advertising has been the biggest single contributor to the rapid economic growth of many key industries like pet foods, which sell their products to a large number of consumers. Through heavy use of TV, today's unfamiliar brand name becomes tomorrow's institution.

Of course, the pet-food war is but one example of thousands of wars being waged for our consumer dollars every day by advertisers. Vance Packard pointed out in *The Hidden Persuaders* that advertisers exploit our fears, hopes, dreams, and anxieties. We must become more aware of this process if we are to make sensible choices about how we spend our money.

Packard feels that advertisers with their "depth manipulation" often make us do things that are irrational and illogical.

> At times it is pleasanter or easier to be nonlogical. But I prefer being nonlogical by my own free will and impulse rather than to find myself manipulated into such acts.
>
> The most serious offense many of the depth manipulators commit, it seems to me, is that they try to invade the privacy of our minds. It is this right to privacy in our minds—privacy to be either rational or irrational— that I believe we must strive to protect.

More recent controversy along these lines has centered on the debate about so-called *subliminal* advertising, or the use of hidden images in magazine and TV ads. A 1973 book exposing this practice, *Subliminal Seduction* by Wilson Bryan Key, stirred quite a response from the industry and the public as well.

Form and Content: How Advertising Works

The effectiveness of advertising is due to the considerable media skills of people in the industry. The cleverest copywriters, best artists, and most talented graphic designers labor over the national advertising campaigns that bombard us. This led Marshall McLuhan to observe: "The ad is the meeting place for all the arts, skills, and all the media of the American environment."

The television-commercial scriptwriter has only 30 seconds to tell the story. Television advertising dispenses with plot line and brings us action and visuals. The scene may shift several dozen times in that 30 seconds. First a close-up of a hand holding a drink—suddenly a plane flies overhead—a flight attendant pours a cup of coffee—a child laughs in glee while being served a hot dog as the clouds roll by outside the window.

Form is the important thing; content is secondary. The ad for a shirt company shows a field of daisies; there's no shirt and no people. The voice-over tells us: "This shirt makes you *feel* like a daisy." It's like Picasso's painting *Man in Chair*. There is no man, no chair, only a collection of skewed lines that represent what it *feels like* to sit in a chair.

Print media, particularly magazines, are replete with examples. A full-page ad for silverware pictures a tree. A Marlboro ad pictures a man herding horses down a hillside. The cigarette packages are almost hidden in the lower right-hand corner, and the rest of the page is devoted to trees and a mountain stream. In another ad, a tiny GM logo is in a lower left-hand corner, and the Chevrolet is unrecognizably dwarfed by a huge canyon. In each case, visual space is given over to a scene that has a minimal "logical" connection with the product. The theory is that by surrounding the product with a pleasant environment, the medium can entice the consumer to try it.

But the consumer is also busy learning other things. Ads tell us a great deal about our society, and they help to influence and change that society. Although the first business of ads is to sell products, their influence doesn't stop there. In fact, that's where it begins. As McLuhan points out, "Advertising itself is an information commodity far greater than anything it advertises." In their rush to sell a product, advertisers sometimes don't even recognize the more important effects of their collective art—selling life-styles and social values to an entire generation of Americans.

Advertising is the first to reflect and encourage social trends. According to McLuhan, advertising "responds instantly to any social change, making ads in themselves invaluable means of knowing where it's at." For example, America's interest in ecology during the 1970s showed up often in advertising: ads featuring the "natural" environment to sell, as noted, everything from cigarettes to silverware. The women's movement had barely gotten started when television ads began picturing women as mechanics and bank presidents. Ads are first to reflect social trends because they *have* to be one step ahead. Competition in advertising is far fiercer than in programming or editorial content, so advertising is often more interesting than the program or article itself.

Advertising also teaches us how to behave through little socialization lessons. As we've noted, ads teach us that if we love our pets, we must feed them a special kind of food. And they teach us how and when to love each other. A wife makes her husband happy by straining his coffee through a special filter. Ads also provide a context and a meaning for all sorts of everyday experiences. A smelly house means social disapproval from important guests.

Issues and Answers: The Selling of the President

Back in 1960, when the role of advertising and PR in politics first became apparent, *Life* magazine quoted one campaign strategist as saying, "I can elect any person to office if he has $60,000, an IQ of at least 120, and can keep his mouth shut."

Since the 1896 campaign, the election of a President has been determined largely by the ability of information specialists to generate favorable publicity. In recent years that publicity has been supplanted by heavy spot buying on electronic media.

The most talked-about medium in American politics is television. Highly publicized debates between candidates in 1960, 1976, and 1980 appear to have affected the outcomes. Richard Nixon (the early favorite) would probably not have lost to John Kennedy were it not for his poor showing on TV. Similarly, the 1976 debates probably clinched Jimmy Carter's narrow victory over Gerald Ford, and Ronald Reagan outshone Carter in the 1980 debates.

Yet there were other elections where, according to political analyst Edward Chester, no amount of TV exposure could have changed the outcome: Barry Goldwater versus Lyndon Johnson in 1964 and Nixon versus George McGovern in 1972. Television commercials seem to work best in close elections or in those where there is a large undecided vote. According to the Associated Press, Ford's TV spots during the 1976 campaign probably swung over 100,000 undecided voters a day during the last few months of the campaign. Nevertheless, he lost the election.

What effect does television have on the candidates themselves? It dictates priorities that are different from those of an earlier day. The physical appearance of the candidate is increasingly important. Does he or she look fit, well-rested, secure? Losing candidates like Adlai Stevenson, Hubert Humphrey, and Richard Nixon all seemed to look "bad" on TV. Nixon overcame this problem in 1972 with ads that featured longer shots of him being "presidential"—flying off to China, for example. Close-ups were avoided.

Both Kennedy and Carter seemed more at home with the medium, perhaps because both were youthful, informal, and physically active outdoor types. Dwight Eisenhower and Lyndon Johnson seemed to have a paternal, fatherly image on the small screen. All of the recent Presidents have learned how to use the medium to their advantage, to "stage" events so as to receive maximum favorable coverage. This has added to the already awesome power of the incumbency.

Television has diminished the significance of issues. It can be argued that since the 1960 presidential debaters, we have elected people, not platforms. This is a major departure from earlier years. Franklin Roosevelt's radio charisma cannot be denied, but he was swept to power by one issue—the Great Depression.

All the print information we now receive is simpler and more condensed than ever before. Issues and print go together. Television is *images*, not issues. We develop a more personal, emotional feeling about the candidates. Jimmy Carter's spectacular rise to power was a testament to this new image orientation. No one really knew *what* he was going to do when he took office, since his entire campaign had been geared toward developing a relationship of trust with the electorate. "Trust me," he said, "I'll never lie to you."

A more recent example was the election of Reagan in 1980. For some, this represented the ultimate television victory. After all, what other country can claim that it has elected an actor President? It can be argued that Americans were tired of Carter and that Reagan simply offered an alternative. Yet throughout the campaign he offered us a media "vision" of a "shining city on a hill." And what about his constant references to John Wayne, one of the "last great Americans"?

My father, a long-time politician in southern California, used to say, "The worst thing a candidate can do is get bogged down in the issues." This trend has alarmed countless media critics. Politicians, newscasters, and others have stood in line to denounce it. They assert that the important thing is *what the candidates stand for,* not the candidates themselves. Almost everyone seems to agree that television has been detrimental to American politics; it has clouded the issues and confused the electorate.

Media researchers Thomas E. Patterson and Robert D. McClure say the power of TV has been overrated and that (1) "Viewers of the nightly network newscasts learn almost nothing of importance about a presidential election," and (2) "People are not taken in by advertising hyperbole and imagery. . . . exposure to televised ads has *no effect on voters' images of the candidates.*" [italics mine] I disagree on both counts.

If the Watergate mess proved anything, it was that we need a President we feel we *know* and can *trust.* Print afforded us no opportunity to get a "feel" for the person. We could study the issues, read the speeches, yes—but how would we "know" the candidate as we might a neighbor or casual acquaintance? Television (and television advertising) provides an audiovisual record of the candidate under all sorts of circumstances. It is with that knowledge that we can choose someone of integrity, at least someone with honorable intentions.

Of course, TV cannot guarantee honest candidates, but we rejected Richard Nixon in 1960 and we might have again had he not so successfully *avoided* any informal coverage. (He wouldn't let TV newscasters near him unless he had a suit on. For all we knew he wore a suit while walking on the beach.) Once he was President, it was the intimate nature of the medium that helped bring him down. Even his well-rehearsed Watergate denials wouldn't work. He would sit there surrounded by flags and piles of transcripts and swear he was innocent. Yet the sweat on his brow and the look in his eyes seemed to confirm his guilt.

Issues come and go, but we elect *people* to the presidency. In this fast-moving information environment, today's burning issue is tomorrow's historical footnote. It's far more important to develop a sense of what kind of person we are electing to the nation's highest office. Television affords us that opportunity in a way no other medium can.

Assignment 5: Presentation in Pairs

1. Prepare an outline of your presentation using Worksheet 3.

2. Prepare two discussion questions and their answers, again using Worksheet 3.

3. In pairs, give your presentation to your partner. Remember, you are the expert. When you have concluded your presentation, ask your partner the two discussion questions you have prepared.

4. Your partner will make suggestions on how your presentation can be improved. Use these suggestions to revise your presentation before you give it to the entire class.

Assignment 6: Seminar: "Television Advertising in America"

1. If possible, students should sit in a large circle.

2. The order of the presentations follows the order of the sections of the article.

3. The first student gives his seminar presentation to the class. That student then leads the class in a discussion using the questions he has written.

4. The teacher will close the seminar by summarizing the important points brought out in the presentations and discussions.

Worksheet 1/Presentation Outline: "Aspects of Education"

Prepare the outline for your talk by using the following format.

Section of the Article: _____

I. Introduction: Identify the central idea.

II. Body: List three main points and their supporting details.

    A.

       1.

       2.

    B.

       1.

       2.

    C.

       1.

       2.

III. Conclusion: Point out how your section fits into the article as a whole.

(Over)

Discussion questions

Write down two discussion questions and their answers that cover your section of the article.

Question #1:

Answer:

Question #2:

Answer:

Worksheet 2/Definitions from "Television Advertising in America"

After you have chosen three terms or phrases from your portion of the article, complete this worksheet.

Definition 1

a. Explain your definition in terms that your classmates will understand. Be sure that your explanation defines the term *as it is used in the article.*

b. Use the term in an original sentence that clearly illustrates its meaning.

Definition 2

a. Explain your definition . . .

b. Use the term in a sentence . . .

Definition 3

a. Explain your definition . . .

b. Use the term in a sentence . . .

Worksheet 3/Presentation Outline: "Television Advertising in America"

Prepare the outline for your talk by using the following format.

Section of the Article: _____

I. Introduction: Identify the central idea

II. Body: List three main points and their supporting details

A.

1.

2.

B.

1.

2.

C.

1.

2.

III. Conclusion: Point out how your section fits into the article as a whole.

Discussion questions

Write down two discussion questions and their answers that cover your section of the article.

Question #1:

Answer:

Question #2:

Answer:

CHAPTER 10

Challenging and Defending a Position

Skills used in this chapter:

— asking and answering questions
— making timed presentations
— analyzing an issue
— collaborating with colleagues
— challenging a position
— defending a position

This chapter reviews some of the most important skills practiced in this textbook: asking and answering questions, analyzing an issue, collaborating with colleagues, and making brief and concise presentations. This chapter also introduces two new skills, challenging and defending a position. All of these skills are practiced in the context of a debate.

What Is a Debate?

A debate is a formal contest in which two teams present opposing arguments on a controversial topic, such as gun control or television violence. The goal of each team is to convince the audience of its point of view, and thus *win* the argument. A debate differs from a simple discussion of a controversial topic in that it has a formal structure that must be followed, it is timed, and there is an audience that observes the debate and chooses a winner. Because the debate is fast paced, it requires quick thinking, precise language, and attentive listening. In colleges and universities, a debate is a contest of students' skills in presentation, argumentation, and logical thinking. At the conclusion of a debate, the audience members vote for the team that presented its position more convincingly.

Why Practice a Debate?

Even though you may never participate in a formal debate during your time at the university, practicing a debate will nonetheless sharpen your ability to speak confidently and clearly. The fact that a debate is timed and places its participants under pressure adds a new dimension to the development of these skills.

What Is the Format of a Debate?

In a debate there are two teams. One team presents arguments in favor of the topic (the Pro Team); the other team presents arguments in opposition to the topic (the Con Team). The teams sit at opposite sides of a table. The moderator (the teacher) sits at the head of the table and times each part of the debate. Two parts of the debate, the introductory and concluding statements, are prepared; a third part, the question and answer period, is spontaneous.

Assignment Overview

You will participate in two debates. The purpose of the first debate is to familiarize you with the style and format of the debate. The second debate is designed to give you an opportunity to put your experience into practice. You will be given one class period to prepare for each debate.

Useful Expressions

There are $\begin{bmatrix} \text{two} \\ \text{three} \\ \text{four} \end{bmatrix}$ main reasons why we take our position:

In the $\begin{bmatrix} \text{first} \\ \text{second} \end{bmatrix}$ place, _____.

To illustrate my point: _____.

For example, _____.

For instance, _____.

Furthermore, _____.

In addition, _____.

This is $\begin{bmatrix} \text{important} \\ \text{obvious} \end{bmatrix}$ because _____.

Let me repeat our position.

In summary, _____.

In conclusion, _____.

I can't go along with that idea.

I don't see it that way.

What you've said isn't accurate because _____.

Yes, but on the other hand, _____.

Assignment 1: Preparing for the Debate

1. Your teacher will divide the class into four teams.

2. Your teacher will then pair the teams off. Each pair of teams must agree on a topic from the list below. Once a topic has been selected by one pair of teams, it cannot be selected by another.

3. The teacher will now decide which team in each pair will be the Pro Team and which will be the Con Team.

4. Spend one class period preparing for the debate.

   a. Choose a team leader.

   b. The team leader will guide a twenty-minute discussion on your team's position. The purpose of this discussion is for your team to identify the major arguments in support of its position. As in any small group discussion, all members should contribute.

   c. Using the arguments generated by the discussion, your team should prepare a four-minute introductory statement that presents the team's position. Use Worksheet 1.

   d. Now discuss the objections the opposing team will probably bring against your arguments and how you will respond to these objections.

   e. Write your comments under number 2 on the same worksheet. Write down your team's objections to the opposing team's likely arguments under number 3 on the worksheet.

5. In your small groups, practice the following in preparation for the debate.

a. The team leader presents the four-minute introductory statement.

b. Team members take turns asking the questions they think the opposing team will ask. Every team member should have an opportunity to ask and answer at least one question.

Topics

Family issues

1. Competition between husband and wife in their careers is healthy for a marriage.

2. A husband and wife should contribute to their expenses in proportion to their earnings.

3. When the husband stays home and does the housework and the wife works to support the family, the family suffers.

4. The husband should manage the family's money.

5. When both husband and wife work full time, the one who earns less should do more housework.

Education

1. College education should be provided only for the very best students.

2. American universities should provide counseling for foreign students to help them adjust to living and studying in the United States.

3. Foreign students studying in the United States should live like Americans.

4. Students majoring in one of the humanities (for example, art, music, literature, languages) do not need to study math and the sciences to be well educated.

5. University professors should be evaluated on their research ability rather than on their teaching ability.

6. Foreign students who need English language instruction should not be admitted to American universities.

7. Tests should not be a part of graduate education, but rather students should be evaluated through papers, presentations, and projects.

Science

1. With the development of science and technology, religion has become obsolete.

2. The sciences are more important to society than the humanities.

3. Scientists should be required to study music, art, and literature.

4. The development of science has harmed society.

5. Pure science should receive more funding than applied science.

6. The current state of world affairs—wars, famine, poverty, the arms race—proves the failure of science to truly improve the lot of mankind.

Social concerns

1. Men are more intelligent than women.

2. Television is harmful to society.

3. Developing nations should change their cultures to make way for modernization.

4. Women are better political leaders than men.

5. The developed countries have a moral obligation to assist the developing countries.

Guidelines for the Debate

Assignment 2: Debate 1

Each debate will take approximately fifty minutes.

Time limits for each section of the debate are to be strictly enforced.

No interruptions are permitted during any part of the debate.

1. The first pair of teams should arrange themselves so that they are facing each other with the moderator (the teacher) at the head of the table. It is the moderator's responsibility to see that time limits are strictly observed and that courteous behavior is maintained throughout the debate.

2. The Pro Team leader presents the team's introductory statement. *Four Minutes.*

3. After the Pro Team has finished its introductory statement, the Con Team asks questions about statements or claims in the Pro Team's introductory statement. These questions should be directed at any weaknesses in the introductory statement. This section

should be fast paced, with concise questions and answers. Any member of the Pro Team may answer a question. *Six minutes.*

4. The procedure is repeated with the Con Team. Introductory statement—*Four minutes;* Question-and-Answer period—*Six minutes.*

5. There is a *five-minute* break during which each team prepares the concluding statement. The concluding statement should not repeat the introductory statement, but it should summarize the team's strongest arguments and should give a sense of completion to the team's position.

6. The Con Team presents its concluding statement. *Two minutes.*

7. The Pro Team closes the debate with its concluding statement. *Two minutes.*

8. At the end of the debate:

   a. Audience members complete Scoresheet 1.

   b. The teacher asks the audience members to say which team they voted for and why.

   c. The teacher then counts the votes and declares one team the winner.

Assignment 3: Debate 2

In this assignment, the winning teams from Assignment 2 will debate each other, and the losing teams from Assignment 2 will debate each other. Choose a new topic from the list in Assignment 1. Prepare for this debate by following the instructions for Assignments 1 and 2. Use Worksheet 2 and Scoresheet 2.

Worksheet 1/Debate 1

Use this worksheet to prepare each section of the debate.

Topic: _____

Position (check one) Pro _____ Con _____

1. *Introductory Statement:* List your team's major arguments.

    a.

    b.

    c.

    d.

2. List questions that you think the opposing team will ask about your introductory statement. Jot down your responses to these questions.

    Questions   *Responses*

    a.

    b.

    c.

3. Write down questions that you might raise against the opposing team's introductory statement.

a.

b.

c.

4. *Concluding Statement:* Summarize your team's *strongest* arguments. You will probably want to revise this during the five-minute break in the debate that precedes the Concluding Statements.

a.

b.

c.

Scoresheet 1/Debate 1

After this debate, complete this scoresheet for both teams. Remember that you are evaluating debating skill, *not* the position being argued. Your teacher will count the votes and declare one team the winner.

Debate 1: Topic _____ Pro _____ Con _____

Rate each team on each category listed below using this scale of 1 to 4.

	Poor			Superior
	1	2	3	4

Pro   Con

_____ _____ A. *Analysis:* The team presented the strongest possible arguments to support its position.

_____ _____ B. *Evidence:* The team supported its arguments with good examples.

_____ _____ C. *Organization:* The team's introductory and concluding statements were clear and well organized.

_____ _____ D. *Questions:* The team's questions (during the six-minute Question period) were concise and exposed weaknesses in the opposing team's arguments.

_____ _____ E. *Answers:* The team's answers to questions were concise and to the point.

_____ _____ F. *Presentation:* The team members communicated their position persuasively by combining delivery, gestures, and eye contact to create an image of competence and leadership.

_____ _____ G. *Participation:* All members of the team participated, by making statements, asking questions of the other team, or answering the other team's questions.

_____ _____ TOTAL

Winner: Pro _____ Con _____

Worksheet 2/Debate 2

Use this worksheet to prepare each section of the debate.

Topic: _____

Position (check one) Pro _____ Con _____

    1. *Introductory Statement:* List your team's major arguments.

       a.

       b.

       c.

       d.

    2. List questions that you think the opposing team will ask about your introductory statement. Jot down your responses to these questions.

      Questions   *Responses*

       a.

       b.

       c.

3. Write down questions that you might raise against the opposing team's introductory statement.

   a.

   b.

   c.

4. *Concluding Statement:* Summarize your team's *strongest* arguments. You will probably want to revise this during the five-minute break in the debate that precedes the Concluding Statements.

   a.

   b.

   c.

Scoresheet 2/Debate 2

After this debate, complete this scoresheet for both teams. Remember that you are evaluating debating skill, *not* the position being argued. Your teacher will count the votes and declare one team the winner.

Debate 2: Topic _____ Pro _____ Con _____

Rate each team on each category listed below using this scale of 1 to 4.

Poor			Superior
1	2	3	4

Pro   *Con*

_____ _____ A. *Analysis:* The team presented the strongest possible arguments to support its position.

_____ _____ B. *Evidence:* The team supported its arguments with good examples.

_____ _____ C. *Organization:* The team's introductory and concluding statements were clear and well organized.

_____ _____ D. *Questions:* The team's questions (during the six-minute Question period) were concise and exposed weaknesses in the opposing team's arguments.

_____ _____ E. *Answers:* The team's answers to questions were concise and to the point.

_____ _____ F. *Presentation:* The team members communicated their position persuasively by combining delivery, gestures, and eye contact to create an image of competence and leadership.

_____ _____ G. *Participation:* All members of the team participated, by making statements, asking questions of the other team, or answering the other team's questions.

_____

_____ _____ TOTAL

Winner: Pro _____ Con _____

APPENDIX

Guidelines for Speaking in Academic Settings

Characteristics of a Good Speaker

Effective communication depends on both form and content: how you say something is as important as what you say. This is particularly true when you are speaking to a group. To ensure effective communication, a presentation should exemplify the following characteristics.

1. Good organization

2. Preparation

   a. Speak from clear and comprehensive lecture notes.

   b. Practice your presentation.

   c. Do *not* read your presentation.

3. Confidence

   a. Do not begin with an apology for your knowledge or your English. If you lack confidence in yourself, the audience will perceive it and lose confidence in you, too.

   b. Be thoroughly prepared and familiar with your material: preparation creates confidence.

4. Responsiveness

   a. Make eye contact with members of the audience. Don't talk to the back wall, the table, or your notes.

   b. Check to see whether the audience is following you.

5. Clarity
   a. Be sure that the organization of your talk is clear to the audience.
   b. Strive for a smooth transition from one point to the next.
   c. Use the blackboard to illustrate and clarify difficult points.

6. Enthusiasm
   a. When something is important, say it slower and louder.
   b. Try to communicate to the audience your own interest in and enthusiasm for your subject: enthusiasm is contagious!

The Interview

If you are the interviewer:

1. You may refer to the list of questions you prepared in Assignment 1.

2. Begin the interview by explaining your purpose.

3. If you do not understand the answer to one of your questions, ask the person to repeat it or clarify it.

4. Try not to talk too much.

5. Let the conversation run naturally. If you think of a new question during the interview, ask it.

6. Take notes during the interview.

7. After the interview, at home, read over your notes and prepare a summary of the interview.

If you are the interviewee:

1. Give complete answers to the questions. Volunteer information.

2. Pay careful attention to the interviewer's questions. If you don't understand one, ask for clarification.

3. Before answering a difficult question, spend a few seconds collecting your thoughts.

Discussions

In a class discussion the entire class participates in a discussion of an article that all class members have read. In most discussions of this type, the teacher asks questions to check your understanding of the article. In America, teachers expect students to take an active role in class by volunteering answers to the questions.

Guidelines for the Group Discussion Leader

The leader bears much of the responsibility for the success of a small group discussion. It is the leader's job to see that all the members participate, that each member has a chance to fully develop his views, that the discussion does not wander from the topic, and that an accurate record of the discussion is kept.

The leader should do the following:

1. Read the question out loud to the group.
    a. Be sure that all the members understand the question.
    b. Provide background information if it is necessary.
2. Guide the discussion.
    a. Let the other members of the group do most of the talking.
    b. Be sure every member has an opportunity to speak without interruption.
    c. Encourage group members to support their opinions with examples from their own experiences.
    d. Be sure the members listen attentively to one another.
    e. Don't let the discussion wander from the topic.
    f. If there is disagreement, make sure it is expressed in a polite and respectful manner.
3. Appoint someone to take notes on the discussion.

Guidelines for the Group Note-Taker

1. Take accurate notes on the discussion.
2. Read your notes out loud to the group at the end of the discussion and make the necessary corrections.
3. Present your summary of the discussion to the entire class.

Guidelines for Group Members

A small group discussion cannot succeed without the cooperation and participation of every member. The appropriate behavior for a group discussion member in the United States is listed below:

1. Do not speak until the leader has recognized you.
2. Do not interrupt another speaker.
3. Support your ideas with information from your own experience.
4. Listen carefully to what the other group members say.
5. Be sure that what you have to say is directly related to the topic.

The Impromptu Speech

The essence of the impromptu speech is the ability to speak confidently and clearly in front of a group with very little preparation. For this reason, you will have only five minutes to prepare your speech. The following steps are essential for a successful impromptu speech:

1. Read your topic carefully.

2. Decide what your position is on the topic. Do you agree or disagree? Then, express your opinion in the form of a statement. For example: "I agree with the idea that the preservation of the natural environment deserves the cooperation of all nations."

3. Write down some notes to help you plan your speech:

   a. Plan your introduction. The simplest introduction is to restate the topic.

   b. Choose two or three examples to support your opinion.

   c. Conclude by repeating your opinion.

The Panel

A panel usually consists of a group of three or four speakers who are experts on various aspects of a single topic, plus a moderator who introduces the speakers. During a panel, each speaker gives a presentation on her area of expertise within a larger topic to an audience of nonexperts. At the conclusion of all of the presentations, a lively question-and-answer period between the audience and the panel members is directed by the moderator.

Panel members prepare their talks on their topics. Remember that an interesting talk is one that includes many specific, relevant examples and draws on personal experience.

Guidelines for the Panel Moderator

1. Introduce all panel members including yourself.

2. Make sure that each speaker stays within the time allotted for each presentation.

3. At the conclusion of the last presentation, invite questions from audience members. It is your job to call on audience members with questions and to decide which panelist(s) will provide answers.

4. Close the panel by announcing the end of the question-and-answer period.

The Seminar

A seminar is a group of students studying under a professor and exchanging information and ideas through reports and discussions.
In many seminars, the students discuss a reading assignment.
Each member of the group gives a report on one aspect of the general topic being discussed and is expected to be able to answer questions about that portion of the topic.

A seminar differs from a panel in that seminar participants are normally classmates, there is no audience in a seminar, and there is no moderator in a seminar.

If you are the presenter:

1. Know *your* section of the article. You are not expected to be an expert on the entire article. For your presentation, summarize the major points of your portion of the reading and define the new words and phrases. During your presentation, you may refer to your notes, but do not read your presentation.

2. Relate your particular part of the reading to the whole reading assignment.

3. After your presentation, lead the class in a short discussion of the ideas covered in your section. Ask the audience questions about concepts, points of view, and implications rather than about simple facts.

If you are a seminar participant:

1. Prepare for the seminar by reading the entire assignment. Be familiar with the major ideas in the reading.

2. Listen to each report carefully. Take notes and write down questions you may have.

3. Participate in the group discussion following a report.

The Debate

A debate is a formal contest in which two teams present opposing arguments on a controversial topic. One team presents arguments in favor of the topic (the Pro Team); the other team presents arguments in opposition to the topic (the Con Team). The teams sit at opposite sides of a table. The moderator (the teacher) sits at the head of the table and times each part of the debate. The goal of each team is to convince the audience of its point of view, and thus *win* the argument. Two parts of the debate, the introductory and concluding statements, are prepared; a third part, the question and answer period, is spontaneous.

A debate differs from a simple discussion of a controversial topic in that it has a formal structure that must be followed, it is timed, and there is an audience that observes the debate and chooses a winner.

Each debate will take approximately fifty minutes.

Time limits for each section of the debate are to be strictly enforced.

No interruptions are permitted during any part of the debate.

1. The first pair of teams should arrange themselves so that they are facing each other with the moderator (the teacher) at the head of the table. It is the moderator's responsibility to see that time limits are strictly observed and that courteous behavior is maintained throughout the debate.

2. The Pro Team leader presents the team's introductory statement. *Four Minutes.*

3. After the Pro Team has finished its introductory statement, the Con Team asks questions about statements or claims in the Pro Team's introductory statement. These questions should be directed at any weaknesses in the introductory statement. This section should be fast paced, with concise questions and answers. Any member of the Pro Team may answer a question. *Six minutes.*

4. The procedure is repeated with the Con Team. Introductory statement—*Four minutes;* Question-and-Answer period— *Six minutes.*

5. There is a *five-minute* break during which each team prepares the concluding statement. The concluding statement should not repeat the introductory statement, but it should summarize the team's strongest arguments and should give a sense of completion to the team's position.

6. The Con Team presents its concluding statement. *Two minutes.*

7. The Pro Team closes the debate with its concluding statement. *Two minutes.*

8. At the end of the debate:
   a. Audience members declare one team the winner.
   b. The moderator asks the audience members to say which team they voted for and why.
   c. The moderator then counts the votes and declares one team the winner.